Out With It

Gay and Straight Teens Write About Homosexuality

By Youth Communication

Edited by Al Desetta

Introduction by Eric Marcus

YOUTH COMMUNICATION

True Stories by Teens

Out With It

Executive Editor
Keith Hefner

Contributing Editors
Clarence Haynes, Rachel Blustain, Andrea Estepa, Philip Kay,
Tamar Rothenberg, Sheila Feeney, Carol Kelly, Katia Hetter,
Kendra Hurley, Kimberly Smith and Mike Fricano

Layout & Design
Efrain Reyes, Jr. and Jeff Faerber

Production Manager
Loretta Chan

Cover Art
Untitled, 8/16/1992, Ink on Paper, 18.875" x 14.25"
© The Estate of Keith Haring

ISBN 978-1-933939-72-8

Second Edition
The first edition of this book, published in 1996,
was edited by Philip Kay, Andrea Estepa, and Al Desetta.

Printed in the United States of America

Youth Communication ®
224 W. 29th St., 2nd fl.
New York, NY 10001
212-279-0708
www.youthcomm.org

Table of Contents

Contents

Contents

Contents

Introduction

By Eric Marcus

Ever wonder what you would say if your sister told you she was gay? Or if you found out that your foster mother was a lesbian? You know that boy at school who acts totally gay? What's he thinking when the other kids go after him? And when he didn't come back one day, where did he go?

Gay, bi, trans, questioning. Everyone pretty much knows someone who is (or maybe one of these terms describes *you*). But do you *really* know much beyond the surface? Have you ever talked to someone who has a gay step-dad? Can you imagine what's going through the mind of a girl when she comes out to her parents? What does a gay guy do when he's got a crush on a classmate who may not even be gay? How does a straight teen resolve the conflict between the bad things her church says about homosexuality and what she knows to be true about her gay friend? And why would a gay person want to kill him—or herself?

In the nearly two dozen essays that follow, written by an amazing range of teens—gay and straight, religious and non-religious, living with their parents or in foster care, black, white,

Hispanic—you get the answers to these questions and a lot more. These writers, all participants in the Youth Communication writing programs in New York City, explain in their own words what their lives are like, what they think of themselves, what they think of their friends, and how they deal with their parents, their foster parents, or the kids they live with in group homes.

I hope you'll take away from these stories what I did: beneath the superficial differences, and despite what society may tell us about those differences, everyone wants to love and be loved just the same. But don't take my word for it. Just turn the page and find out.

Eric Marcus is the author of What if Someone I Know Is Gay?, Is It a Choice?, and other books. For more information, see www.ericmarcus.com.

Elizabeth Deegan

I Am Religious, Outgoing, African-American, Talented—and Gay

By Anonymous

When I was 12 or 13 years old, I had my first big crush on another girl. I thought Nicolle was incredibly cute and I wanted to date her. I liked Nicolle's style and the way she carried herself.

Plus, she had a really welcoming grin—like the grin of the most popular boy in a book about high school. She carried herself in a "no nonsense" type of way. No one picked on her and she never picked on anyone else. People liked her. She was studious, which was cool, and she also loved basketball. She always played with the boys while I played badminton. I admired her for all the shots she made that the guys did not.

I wasn't a good friend with Nicolle, but we'd chat sometimes or joke around. I can't pinpoint exactly when I started liking her, but I can always remember glancing at her in class. Or smiling at her when we made eye contact. And if she smiled back at me, which she always did, that was a bonus. It made me feel good to have somebody I liked give me that kind of attention.

Once, she invited me to her house and I kept wishing she would kiss me. I never told her that because I thought she would react weirdly. I thought she might hit me or tell me to get out of her house. Or even worse, she might totally think I was joking. So I never did tell her how I felt.

Even though I wasn't comfortable telling her, I was not surprised about my feelings for her. I thought it was OK to like someone, male or female. It was just another crush to me.

I knew what gay people were at a young age and I never thought they were weird. At age 8 or 9, my aunt had a gay friend who she told me about. I took it in stride. Occasionally there were people who did not care much for gay people. Generally, though, people around me were more positive than negative. Probably because of that, I was open-minded at a young age. I thought both females and males were beautiful. I thought women were sexy.

Still, I did not immediately come out to myself or to anyone else after I realized my attraction to females. I felt comfortable liking who I liked and I didn't feel the need to start calling myself by another name to identify myself. I did not even know that a girl who liked girls called herself a lesbian or a bisexual. I just knew my feelings.

But last year, in October, I finally did come out. I joined a teen support group for gay, lesbian, transgendered, questioning, bisexual, and non-labeling youth.

Being in the group made me realize that I was part of a somewhat segregated community, and I wanted to let people know that I was proud to be gay and that I didn't want to hide it. First I came out as bisexual, but later I decided that I only wanted to be with other girls.

I was 16 at the time and I was so happy with myself. I told many of my friends what I knew about myself, and my true friends took it well. I only had a few bad cases.

The hardest person to come out to has been my mom.

I decided not to tell my friend Dede, because, when I brought up gay people in conversation, she told me that she didn't like lesbians. I was disappointed by her answer and I started drifting away from her.

My 10-year-old sister was the first person I told in my family.

"Sarah, do you know what a gay person, a lesbian, and a bisexual are?" I asked her.

"Yeah."

"What's a bisexual?"

"I don't know."

"That's a person who likes males and females. They might also have sex with them. OK?"

"Yeah."

Then I said, "Sarah, I'm bisexual. Do you still love me?"

"Of course I do," she said. "I don't care what you are,"

Then I gave her a hug in the middle of the street. At that moment it didn't matter whether or not the rest of my family accepted me. By opening up to my sister, I felt I paved my way for coming out to the "world."

I told my other siblings (all younger than me, but older than my little sister) a few months later when they kept teasing me and getting on my nerves. I just blew up at them and told them the truth. They started bugging. My sister threw pencils at me and kept saying she didn't believe me.

My brother kept asking me, "Was that girl who slept over your girlfriend? You don't like boys at all?"

But after a few days they calmed down. I guess I knew that they accepted me when they asked me how I knew I liked girls, if I had a girlfriend, and who was the man and the girl in the relationship. The questions went on for two or three days. By the time I got a girlfriend in May, it was no longer an issue.

The hardest person to come out to has been my mom. She hasn't been bad, but she hasn't been totally accepting, either. When I first told her I was bisexual, she told me that she still loved me, and then she gave me a hug and kiss on the cheek. I was pleased about that.

But then she said, "Everybody goes through it. It's just a phase." Then she left and I was speechless. I felt betrayed.

The next day I started going out with my first girlfriend. I met her at a meeting for youth from the gay community. I told my mom immediately so she wouldn't be surprised. She didn't take it as well as I expected, but she dealt with it. I invited my mom into my bedroom and said, "Mom, I have something to tell you."

In a wary voice she said, "Don't tell me about your friend. I don't want to know."

"I just want you to know that we're girlfriends."

I don't remember what we said after that but I think she asked me something about whether we were having sex. I said no. She left with a smile on her face.

For a while after that, I didn't feel like I could really talk to my mom. She would ask me whether I was gay or bisexual, or how long it was going to last, and I'd get annoyed. Then we had a conversation and she explained how she felt.

Right now she says she doesn't mind my sexuality. But as a Christian, she wants me to have a close relationship with God, and she says that eventually I'm going to have to decide between my sexuality and God. She says it's either/or.

She still says she supports me no matter what and she even

inquires about my girlfriend. But she also gets annoyed if I bring up her name. She let me go to a camp for gay teens, but she doesn't like my gay friends sleeping over. And somehow I don't think my mom believes that gay people can be in love with each other.

My mom wants me to know that she cares about my happiness, and she lets me know that she loves me daily. But I also know that she thinks I can only be close to God if I decide to be straight. (I was raised very religiously, and actually, that's the one thing I'm still struggling with.)

I haven't been that close to my mom for a while. And since I told her I'm gay, we've grown even more distant. That hurts. And it makes it even more important for me to have other people around who support me. Two of them are Contessa (the sweetest, most beautiful aunt) and Ms. James (a loving second mother to me, and adult confidant).

One day, sometime in July or August of this year, I had a really short chat with Ms. James. It went like this.

I whispered, "Do you know I have a girlfriend?"

She didn't hear me, so I said, "Do you know that I'm gay?" Then I stepped back to look at her face.

She laughed and said, " Yes. It's OK with me, baby. I don't mind. You are still doing good."

Telling my Aunt Contessa was just as nice. When I told her how I felt, she said, "I respect that and I respect you. It's good that you know what you want. When I was about your age, I thought I might have been bisexual. But I figured out I wasn't. It is good that you know and you tell people."

Another thing that has helped me was going to a camp for gay teens for the last week in August. It was so cool. We were near a lake, so I was able to swim and boat. We had campfires, good food, heartfelt group discussions, arts and crafts, games, prizes, a talent show, a dance, a beautiful history lesson about being gay, hacky sack, laughs, cries, scares, powerful rain, blown out lights, and utter fun. We even went swimming at night under a sky full of stars. It was a blast.

This camp was geared to helping gay youth keep a positive attitude about themselves and building small family groups among us. It was a camp for empowering the youth of the gay community. It helped me and a lot of other youth share ourselves and feel safe and accepted.

I'm gay, but I still feel the way I've always felt most of the time: content, happy, in love, solid, whole, loved, pressed for time, and loving life. Being gay is just a part of who I am. I am also religious, outgoing, talented, young, pretty, short, African-American, friendly, caring, loving, peaceful, focused, proud, and honest. And I love country music.

> Being gay is part of who I am. I don't feel I should stand apart from others because of my sexuality.

I don't feel like I should stand apart from others because of my sexuality. It feels weird if I do. Gay people are no different from the rest of the world and we should not be ridiculed, bashed, fired, looked down upon, feared, or unloved.

When I tell people that I'm gay, I'm not trying to "flaunt it" or throw it in their faces. I just hope that if I make people aware of who I am, they may think twice about their beliefs.

But sometimes I don't tell people I'm gay and I wish I had. The other day in school, just as I was finishing talking to two of my gay male friends, I overheard another boy say to his friend in a surprised tone, "There's two gay kids!"

As I passed them, I said, "So?"

When I turned around, the two guys were looking at me. So I said with a wave of my hand, "You don't have to worry about them."

I was trying to tell them not to bother the gay kids, but it sounded like I was saying my friends wouldn't try to "rap" to them if they knew they were straight (which is true). Instead, I wished I had said, "So? I'm gay too, and those are my friends." I wish I had stuck up for us and shown that we're proud.

Still, sometimes I get tired of having to tell people that I'm gay. After all, being "gay" is not all we are. It's only a part of us. So if people tell you they're gay, maybe you can ask them what else they are, like an artist or an athlete or a poet.

Being gay is not my lifestyle. It is a part of my life. I love who I am. And I would be pleased if everyone else could accept me, too.

The author was 18 when she wrote this story.

Julio Juarez

Out, Without a Doubt

By Xavier Reyes

Growing up, I always believed negative stereotypes about gays and lesbians. These stereotypes put down homosexuals and gave me an excuse to not educate myself about them. But when I got older, I learned that the only person I was dogging was myself.

When I was 12, I always acted macho and dogged females and gays so my boys wouldn't think that I was a "faggot." We always joked around about "dropping the soap" and never exchanged anything more than just a handshake. I always thought that if two guys exchanged something more than that, something was wrong.

I was extremely homophobic. I believed all the lies that I heard about gays—they're not real men, they're sex maniacs, and they're all going to hell. Anytime my friends and I saw a gay person, we'd make fun of them by trying to walk "feminine."

But when I was 13, my feelings began to change. For example, I once found myself looking at another guy and saying, "Damn, he's cute." When this happened, I tried telling myself that it was wrong. I ignored my feelings and they went away—or at least I thought they did.

When I was 14, the feelings came back stronger. I thought that it was just a phase, so I continued dating girls and putting down gays. But at the same time I kept scoping out other men. I still believed that there was no way in hell that I could be gay. After all, I didn't act like it.

It wasn't until I moved into a foster care group home that I had my eyes opened. I was now 15 and still homophobic. When I first moved in I knew there were gays there, but never expected to have one as my roommate. Because I had allowed myself to fall for myths about gays, I was extremely insecure about having a gay roommate.

I wouldn't change my clothes in front of Mike, I began to sleep in more than just my boxers, and I never walked around in just a towel. I was scared that Mike might try to hit on me or give me a surprise "wake up call" in the middle of the night and make me less of a man.

This insecurity didn't last too long because I began to get to know Mike for who he was, not what he was. I found out that we liked the same music and loved going clubbing. I didn't feel like I had to prove something in order to get his respect. But when Mike asked me if I was straight or gay, I lied and told him that I was straight but had a couple of gay friends.

The reality was that I was lying to myself. I knew I had feelings for guys, but I just didn't want to come out with it. I was afraid of being put down because of it. I didn't want people to think that I was a sissy, but at the same time I felt miserable. I was sacrificing being happy for keeping up my reputation.

After getting to know Mike better, I felt a little more comfortable with my sexuality. I didn't have to put up a front when I was with him. I grew jealous of Mike because he didn't care what people thought of him. His motto was "You get what you give." I wanted to be like him—out and without a doubt. I didn't want to live my life in a closet.

As much as I wanted to come out and be free, I still had a hard time accepting the fact that I was gay. I couldn't picture myself sleeping with another guy. I had always believed that straight men had to act masculine, play sports, and lie about how many girls they had sex with. They didn't have sex with each other. If a guy was gay, then he had to be extremely flamboyant and feminine.

For some reason, Mike didn't seem to fit any of the stereotypes I had. He wasn't flamboyant or feminine. Then it hit me. I realized that I had prejudices about gays and lesbians and, until I was able to free myself from them, I couldn't accept myself.

I had feelings for guys, but I just didn't want to come out with it.

Mike really opened my eyes and mind. I now knew that I didn't have to be feminine. After about three weeks, I decided I was ready to unlock all the locks.

I called Mike into the bedroom and told him that there was something that I had to tell him. I was a nervous wreck. I had sweaty palms, shaky knees, and a dry mouth. He saw how nervous I was and immediately closed the door and asked me what was the matter.

"Mike, I want to tell you something. Please don't tell anyone yet. Okay?"

"Okay," he replied with a concerned expression.

"I, I, I'm, well there's a chance that..."

"What is it?" he asked, getting more and more anxious.

"Well, I could be, you know..."

"Know what?" he asked.

"I might be..."

He looked at me with this "I know you're gay" look and asked me to finish.

"I'm, well, uhm, I'm gay."

I swear, the minute I said that, I felt so relieved. I finally felt like I had no more hidden secrets. It's strange, but it felt like I was even able to breathe a little bit easier now that I had gotten this off my chest.

First Mike laughed, then he looked at me.

"Oh, I knew that," Mike said with his usual "I know everything" tone of voice. "I was just waiting to see when you were going to come out."

Why should I have to be fem just because I'm gay?.

I looked at him and said, "Then how come you never told me?"

His reply was, "I don't know."

Mike was the first person I told I was gay. He promised not to tell anybody else. And I didn't tell anybody else for a couple of days. I was still trying to accept who I was. Just thinking about having a boyfriend or lover made me shake my head in disbelief because I was going against everything that I thought I had believed in.

About a week later I came out to a couple of more people. I always received replies like, "You're gay? No way!," "It's about time," and "You need to get a man." Because my gay friends were supporting me, I decided to take my chances and tell a straight female friend.

"You're what?" Mary asked in disbelief.

"I'm gay," I repeated.

"Boy, you need to stop playing."

"I ain't playing," I replied. "I'm dead up."

She looked at me and said, "You ain't one of 'em 'cause you

don't act like it."

"Act like what?" I asked. By this time she was really pissing me off.

"You know," she said, putting her hand on her hip. "Fem."

"Just because I'm gay doesn't mean that I've got to act fem," I said.

"Well, in my book you do 'cause guys like you aren't gay."

I looked at her and walked away.

When I thought about it later on that night, I kept asking myself, "Why should I have to be fem just because I'm gay?" I finally made up my mind that I was going to be me, regardless of what anybody said. No one could tell me how to act.

I began hanging out with my gay friends more often. We went to clubs, the Village (a neighborhood in New York City where a lot of gay people live), and lots of gay house parties. I met a lot of kids who were my age and who were out of the closet. Some were extremely feminine while others were straight up ruffnecks. Either way, I grew really confident with myself.

When I came out to the staff in the group home, they couldn't believe it. One staff member even said, "A good-looking guy like yourself is gay? Boy, I hope there are some men left out there for my daughter."

It seemed like the more I told people, the more I wanted to come out.

Eventually, I made sure that the whole world knew. I didn't want to live my life in a closet. I had pride in who I was. The only person who didn't know was my adoptive mother.

My adoptive mother and I have always had a bad relationship. It was so bad that I ran away from home when I was 13. Growing up, my adoptive mother spoke badly about gays. She used to say that they needed mental help, that it was immoral to be gay, and that it was "just a phase." To make matters worse, she is a Roman Catholic who strongly believes that homosexuality is a sin. Believe me, I was not running to tell her any time soon that I was gay.

It was very easy for me to avoid having to come out to my adoptive mother. I hardly spoke with her or saw her since I went into a foster care group home. When I was 17, I went AWOL from the group home and moved in with a friend of mine. My friend was also gay but he was much older than I was—19 years older, to be exact.

The agency called my adoptive mother to let her know that I had left care to live on my own. My adoptive mother, of course, wanted to know where I was and who I was with. The agency gave her my telephone number and she called me.

"Hello," I asked, trying to shake the effects of deep sleep from my head.

"Xavier, this is your mother!" she screamed at me.

"Oh," I said holding the phone away from my ear. "Hello mom."

I sat up in bed while preparing my verbal weapons just in case there was an attack from the enemy lines.

"Do you know what the hell you're doing?" she asked, her voice higher than it was before.

"Here we go," I mumbled to myself.

"What!?" she screamed into my ear.

"Listen ma, this is my life," I screamed back at her. "You can't tell me what to do anymore. I don't wanna be in care. I'm tired of being in a group home. I can take care of myself." I was shocked that I actually yelled back for once.

"Well, who are you living with?" she asked. I could tell she was taken back by my tone of independence.

"A friend, ma," I replied, trying to figure out where she was going with her questions.

"I don't know about you. But I find it pretty strange that a 17-year-old is living with a 36-year-old man!" she screamed at me.

"Ma! What do you want? So what if he's 36?" I replied.

"Is he doing anything to you?" she asked. By this time I was really upset with her.

"No, he's not doing anything to me," I said.

"Then why would a 36-year-old take in a 17-year-old?"

I thought about it for a second, then said, "He didn't take me in. I have to pay rent and pay bills just like anyone else would."

"Are you a homosexual?" she asked.

I almost dropped the damn phone on my foot. That was the one thing that I hated about my adoptive mother. She was so blunt and straightforward.

"Am I what?" I asked, trying to get out of telling her the truth.

"Are you a ho-mo-sex-u-al?" she said, sounding out the word as if I was learning it for the first time.

I paused for a minute, debating whether or not I should tell her. I was mad scared but I felt that this would prove to her that I was my own person. I knew that there was only so much thinking that I could do, so I let my mouth make the decision.

My adoptive mother tried dissing me by telling me that I'm not a real man.

"Yes, I am a homosexual, " I said, emphasizing the word.

After I told my adoptive mother I was gay, she tried to tell me that I needed help. I, of course, pointed out that homosexuality was not a mental disorder. Then she tried telling me how society wouldn't accept me. I told her I didn't care what society accepts. After that, she tried dissing me by telling me that I'm not a real man. I told her straight up:

"Mom, the last time I checked below my belly button, everything was still intact. Who I decide to sleep with is my business, not yours. As long as I'm not sleeping with anybody you know, that part of my life has nothing to do with you."

She hung up on me.

Although my adoptive mother wasn't accepting of the fact that I was gay, I still felt relieved that I told her. I had no more secrets from her and she knew who I really was. I wasn't bothered by her homophobia. We didn't have a relationship before I came out, so it really didn't matter if we still didn't have one after I came out.

I moved back into the group home about a month later. It took three months for my adoptive mother to speak to me again. Although we still don't have a close relationship, she has come to accept me. She has told me that she is extremely old-fashioned and she knows that things have changed. She had also told me that there's nothing she can do to change my sexuality and that she has no choice but to accept it.

We had that talk eight months ago. Now she has taken the easy way out: don't ask, don't tell. Whenever I do talk to her nowadays, she doesn't ask, say, or even suggest anything about me being gay. It bothers me that she does this, but I also understand that she has accepted me for who I am.

Out of all the things that I've learned, the most important thing is that I cannot allow any kinds of stereotypes or prejudices to come between me and the rest of the world. I've learned the hard way that I should never judge a book by its cover. Ever since I've come out, I try to get to know people for who they are, not what they are.

I'm not scared anymore to tell people I'm gay. In fact, I enjoy telling them because I don't fit the stereotypes that people have about gays, and that really makes them stop and think twice. I never know when I might bump into someone who could be going through what I went through. The least that I can do for them is be out of the closet.

Xavier earned a college degree in public affairs from Baruch College in New York City. He has worked in philanthropy and the media.

She's Cool, She's Funny, She's Gay— and She's My Sister

By Sandra Leon

When I was younger, I never really cared about what other people had to say about homosexuals. But ever since my sister Sonia came "out of the closet," I've been outspoken on the topic. Now I can't let the dumb remarks about gay people go by without commenting on them.

I always knew my sister Sonia was a lesbian and it never bothered me. But when she finally told my mother, we thought mom was going to scream at the top of her lungs. My mother raised us to think homosexuality was wrong and strange. She totally hated it. I thought mom would disown Sonia or try to force her to be straight.

She did neither. Instead, she withdrew from my sister's life. For a couple of weeks my mother totally ignored Sonia. There was always tension in the air—my mom and Sonia repelled each other. Say my mom was going to the kitchen and Sonia was leaving at the same time. They would meet and then do a 180 to avoid each other. My mom wouldn't step into the kitchen unless Sonia wasn't there and Sonia wouldn't leave the kitchen unless she was 100% sure mom wasn't outside in the hallway.

Then one day my sisters and I were discussing a problem Sonia was having with her first lesbian relationship. My mother overheard and asked us what we were talking about. My little sister said bluntly, "Oh nothing, just that Sonia's got woman troubles." My mother's mouth opened wide but she didn't say a word. She just gave Sonia a how-could-you-talk-to-your-sisters-about-that look.

That night, my sisters and I told mom how we felt about Sonia's sexuality. It took a long time but we finally got through to her. At the end of the discussion, mom told Sonia that even if she didn't agree with what Sonia "chose" to be, she would always love her.

My mom also told Sonia that whenever she had a problem she could always come to her and talk about it. Sonia can openly talk to my mother when she's hurting, no matter what she's hurting about.

I think it's great the way my mother has come to accept Sonia for who she is. Now I'm trying to get my friends to do that too. They're always asking me, "Why is she gay?" and "How does it feel to have a lesbian sister?" Then they want to tell me how they feel about gay people.

So every time I bring friends to my house, Sonia is the first person I introduce them to. When we leave, I tell them, "That's my sister who's gay." Some of my friends just say, "Oh, she's the one? Well, she's nice." But others do a double-take: "That's her? No way, get out of here, really?!"

The people who are surprised tell me that Sonia doesn't look gay or that she doesn't act like a gay person. I reply, "What does a lesbian person look like? How are they supposed to act?" After that, all they have left to say is: "Well, you know." I tell them, "No, I don't know" and ask them to explain themselves.

As a result, I've gotten into some heavy conversations about gay stereotypes with my friends. I couldn't believe some of the ideas they had about gay people. They told me that lesbians dress and look masculine. That they act like men because that's what they want to be. Since my sister isn't like that, she couldn't be gay as far as they were concerned.

I tell them that their stereotypes just aren't true. As far as I know, my sister loves being a woman. She enjoys her femininity. For her, being gay doesn't have anything to do with a secret desire to be a man—far from it. Sonia is a lesbian because she enjoys the company of other women, physically as well as mentally. She's told me that, for her, a relationship between two women is deeper than that between a woman and a man.

Mom told Sonia that even if she didn't agree with what Sonia "chose" to be, she would always love her.

Another thing that a lot of my friends believe is that gay people try to get straight people to become gay. Once a friend asked if she could stay at my house for a couple of days. I told her she could stay as long as she wanted, but she must be comfortable with my sister. She said, "OK, as long as Sonia doesn't fall in love with me." I thought that was a very stupid thing for her to say. My sister doesn't chase after straight women. So I replied with sarcasm: "You're not her type. So please, darling, don't flatter yourself."

Some of my friends also feel that gay people have a negative view of the opposite sex. Not true. My sister has always had men for best friends. She may not be attracted to them sexually but that doesn't mean that she hates men.

I've found that a lot of people who condemn discrimination based on race or religion or nationality act like discrimination against gay people is acceptable. Why is that? How can you be open-minded about one aspect of a person and close-minded about another? Even people who have been victims of discrimination themselves can be totally insensitive when it comes to gay people.

I don't understand people like that, but I can give them a piece of advice: open your eyes and ears, your minds, and your hearts. My mother has and so have a lot of my friends. Knowing Sonia has taught them that you can't believe stereotypes.

Sandra was 17 when she wrote this story. She majored in English and American Literature at New York University.

Mariet Guerrero

My Boy Wanted a Boyfriend

By Odé A. Manderson

One time I was within earshot of a conversation between two older guys and one of them had a friend who revealed he was gay. The dude responded by saying:

"I oughta kick your gay butt for telling me that. Get outta here."

Even though I'm straight, it makes my stomach turn to hear comments like that. Why would someone go out of their way to hate on people because of how they live their lives? I think it's an exercise in stupidity. But I don't feel comfortable going up to strangers and calling them out.

Still, I admit that I've used the word "fag" when I've wanted to insult someone's intelligence. No, I don't think gays are dumb,

but it's a popular slang word. I know it's hypocritical and I'm trying to stop using the term, but old habits die hard.

And even though I don't consider myself to be homophobic, I
used to think that gays act only one way because of how they're
portrayed on TV and film. The actors who portray gays play it
to the hilt with their bold sexual statements, style of dress, and
comments about their gayness. Since I didn't usually run into
anybody who acted in this way, I thought that gays would never
cross my path. It was almost like they lived in a separate world.

I now realize I've probably been in contact with gays and
didn't know it. In high school, my guidance counselor/college
advisor mentioned in an off-hand manner during an assembly
that he was gay. I didn't think too much about it, though. I still
didn't think that I would ever meet someone like me, but gay.

Then, during my stint working in a summer jobs program
two years ago, I met Thomas. On my first day of work he
introduced himself to me and quickly became a good friend. He
was different and cool. I learned a lot from him, like how to take
action when times called for it and to speak my mind a lot more.
He had a sense of humor, and he was straightforward about
everything.

Evidently, he found me equally cool to be around. We started
to hang out on the weekends. Sometimes we chilled at the mall.
Other times we would hang out at a diner after picking up
our paychecks. Or we would go to his cousin's crib, where we
watched cable or listened to music.

When we were hanging out, I picked up on some signs that
made me think Thomas might be gay, like the feminine quality
of his voice and the way his hips swung back and forth when he
walked. But I didn't want to jump to conclusions, so I never said
anything about it. You can't tell someone's sexuality that easily. I
couldn't assume Thomas was gay unless I heard it come straight
from his mouth.

I didn't let it become a big issue with me. We were cool, so it didn't matter.

But toward the end of July, Thomas started to spend more time alone. He went from being outspoken to quiet, and I started to wonder what was going on. I came home from work one day and the phone rang. It was him.

"What the hell is the matter with you?" I demanded. "Dyin' or something?"

He started to say something smart, but stopped. He sighed, then put down the receiver. A few seconds later someone picked it up.

"Hello?"

It was one of his cousins.

"Look," she started. "Thomas has something to say to you, but he's too shy to say it. Do you know what it is?"

I wasn't a total idiot. Or so I thought.

I thought that gays would never cross my path. It was almost like they lived in a separate world.

"Does it have anything to do with his sexual identity?" I asked calmly.

"Yes it does. That's not all, though. The reason why he had a hard time telling you was because he has a crush on you."

I was shocked. Butterflies suddenly fluttered in my gut, then turned into wild hornets bursting through the wall of my stomach. I was silent for a moment before I decided to say something. I was prepared to hear him tell me he was gay, not that he had it for me.

His cousin said that he liked me because of my looks and personality. I blinked hard.

"Tell him he has nothing to be shy about," I replied, trying to compose myself. "Put him on the phone."

I heard a faint "here" as she passed the receiver to Thomas.

"Yeah."

"That's all you had to tell me? Look, you didn't have to tell me anything, so trusting me with that was strong of you. And this won't change our friendship, if that's what you're thinking. I'm cool."

Right after I hung up the phone with Thomas, I called my good friend Darnell because I needed some feedback and advice. The minute I explained what happened, he burst out laughing.

"Odé, that's the worst. He's in love with you, baaaaaa-beeeeeeeeee...." Then added coldly: "I would've screamed on him."

"For what?" I said. "He knows where I stand, so it's not a problem. Plus, he's peoples."

"True, true," Darnell said. "I still would've screamed on him."

But I didn't want Thomas to feel bad that he'd told me. After hearing how kids our age treat gays—the threats, the jokes, and the violence—he was probably scared that I'd go and wild out.

After that, we still hung out as before, even though we didn't talk about his sexual identity or his crush on me again. I didn't want to bring anything up. I was thinking of how I would take it if I were gay and a straight friend started asking me about it. I thought that would make me feel uncomfortable. I didn't want to risk saying something stupid that would make Thomas feel uncomfortable.

I wanted to know if he was happy with himself, even though other people probably didn't accept him because he was gay. But I didn't ask. I didn't want to make him feel like he was on trial for being who he was. I also wondered if he still had a crush on me.

Knowing a guy had feelings for me was unsettling. When girls liked me, I felt a sense of satisfaction. But with Thomas, I felt bewildered. The idea of any guy liking me caught me off guard. This was a new experience and I felt uncomfortable. At the summer job where we worked, a lot of the employees caught on to Thomas' feminine mannerisms.

"Is he gay?" female counselors would ask me. Since I hung

out with him, they turned to me for info.

"Yo, is that guy gay or somethin'?" the male counselors would ask. Then, answering themselves aloud, they'd add in disgust, "Yeah, he's gay." Most people only want to know if someone is gay so they can go in for the attack.

Because of attitudes like that, I think that gay teens are forced to live life differently than straight teens. They have to be careful about what they say and do in front of other people. So I tried to be very respectful of who Thomas was, even though I wasn't perfect at it. And Thomas would sometimes bring up stuff on his sexuality. Those talks let me know where he was coming from.

The idea of any guy liking me caught me off guard and I felt uncomfortable.

One time we started discussing relationships and we swapped stories. He said he had been involved in long-term relationships and his boyfriends were usually four to five years older than him. He talked about how guys treated him and how he felt about the person he was dating, but he didn't go into too much detail. I didn't ask for more information because I didn't want to overstep my boundaries as a friend, and I think he knew that.

For the rest of August, we hung out as much as we used to before Thomas came out. The only time I felt uncomfortable was when I let my tongue slip and used the word "fag" around him. I wanted to kick myself because I didn't know how Thomas took it. It didn't seem to bother him, and that really threw me off. It made me feel stupid, because I knew it was disrespectful. I think he understood that when I used the term it wasn't directed at him. Nevertheless, I didn't want to seem insensitive to him.

After a while I stopped wondering if he still had a crush on me. It didn't matter. Even if he still had feelings for me, it wasn't changing our friendship. But when the summer ended, we didn't keep in touch. A few weeks later, I began lifeguard training and went back to school and dated a few girls. He was trying to get a good job. We weren't able to chill as much because we had less time. After school started, he called twice to see how I was doing but he didn't ask to hang out. Neither did I. I figured he just didn't want to hang out anymore. I don't know why.

Even though we're not friends anymore, I'm glad that Thomas had the guts to come out. I'm impressed that he kept it real and revealed who he was. And our friendship showed me how my perceptions of gay people were pretty off. In reality, signs of gayness are nowhere near as cut and dried as they seem on TV because gay people don't all act the same.

Thomas made me realize that gay people aren't that different from straight people and can't be stereotyped. Thomas had some of the stereotypes in the way he walked and talked, but he was also quiet and thoughtful. He wasn't loud at all. He couldn't even tell me about his sexuality himself.

I've realized I don't live in a separate world from gay people and I don't want to discriminate against them. Ten years from now a gay person could be my boss or my son's godfather. For all I know, my son could be gay. And I wouldn't love him any less.

Odé was 17 when he wrote this story. He attended college and majored in writing.

Kelly Viechweg

What Would You Do
If I Were Gay?

By Gina Trapani

I remember sitting on the couch next to my dad watching the news on television when I was about 10 years old. There was a report on about a gay and lesbian parade. I didn't know what it meant to be gay, so I asked my father and he told me: "That's when two men or two women love each other like a boy and girl do."

"Why would someone want to do that?" I asked.

Without looking at me, he answered, "Well, they can't help it. Gay people are just born like that, like having brown eyes."

"Oh," I said, thinking that it sounded really weird. But then I became worried. What if I turned out be gay? So I said to my dad, "What would you do if I was gay, daddy?" He looked at me and said, "Why?!"

"I was just wondering," I replied, sorry that I had asked at all.

"Well, you would still be my daughter," he said. But for some reason his answer didn't make me feel any better.

A few years later, during my freshman year in high school, I met Jennifer. We became very close, but I knew that the way I felt about her was very different than the way I felt about my other close friends. I was very possessive of Jennifer and didn't want to share her with anyone else. At times I even felt jealous of the guys that she liked.

I learned that I had to be very careful about who I told and who I couldn't tell.

Soon I began to realize that I liked her as more than just a friend. It was very scary for me to think about it, because I'd heard how the girls in school talked about "lezzies" and the disgusting things they did. It was hard to figure out whether or not I was just confused, or if I really was a l-e-s...

Yuck, I couldn't even say the word.

That summer, because I couldn't handle the feelings I was having, I ended my friendship with Jennifer. I never told her why. But I still felt that I had to tell someone what was going on. I decided on my friend Linda, who I looked up to like an older sister. Sitting in her room one day, I sort of hinted around the subject, trying to find out what she thought. I was so afraid that she was going to squeal the minute I brought it up. But she didn't. She looked at me very carefully and intently and waited for me to finish.

Finally I just spit it out: "Linda, what would you think if I, uh, said that I, um, if I liked, I mean like, another girl?" There was a moment's pause. I was dying of embarrassment, very ashamed of what I had told her and very afraid of her reaction.

But she said, "No, no, that's not gross at all."

"Really?!" I said, hoping that she meant it.

"Yes," she told me. "Do you want to talk?" That day Linda made me feel much better. She told me that I wasn't bad or disgusting, and that it was OK to feel that way. For me, that was the first time I ever admitted to myself and another person how I felt. (About a year later, I was not surprised to find out that Linda was a lesbian herself.)

Even though speaking to Linda made me feel better, there were many times when I felt really down and isolated. I didn't know anyone else in the world who was gay or who had even questioned themselves. I was afraid to tell anyone in school. I felt very left out because I didn't have a boyfriend and my friends would always be talking about guys—who they liked and who they were taking to the prom. I didn't belong with them because I wasn't a part of that world and didn't want to be.

Marilyn and Elaine were my two best friends. We'd been in school together since first grade. They were always there for me and always understood me when I had a problem. I was sure that after they got used to the idea they would open up to me and everything would be the same as it had always been between us. So I just said straight out, "I think that I'm a lesbian."

They were shocked. They asked me a couple of questions. But after that one time, they never mentioned it again. Soon we started to talk less and less about anything at all. I don't know if who I am caused that to happen. But I do know that it made me feel really bad. I learned the hard way that they weren't my real friends, and I also learned that I had to be very careful about who I told and who I couldn't tell.

It was, and still is, very frustrating for me to have to live a lie out of fear of other people's reactions. As a result, I began to really appreciate the few people I could tell—all of whom were straight. But I felt like they couldn't really understand because they hadn't experienced it. Finally I decided that it was time I went out and found people that I could talk to and who would truly understand how I felt: other gays and lesbians my age.

I remember standing outside the door of a drop-in center for gay teens in Greenwich Village, a neighborhood in New York City where lots of gay people live. I was afraid to go inside. I had no idea what to expect and I was petrified that I wouldn't fit in there, either.

Finally, I just walked in. A funny-looking girl wearing a base-ball cap came up to me and said, "Hi, I'm Marie." Marie became one of my best friends—a real best friend, because I know that she loves me for who I am, completely.

A couple of months ago, Marie told me about a group that was forming for lesbian and bisexual women who are under 21. The next week I went to one of their meetings and the women there made me feel right at home. It felt great to be able to goof around with them, joking about ourselves and the people around us. If I talked like that with my straight friends they wouldn't understand. Ever since that first meeting, I've gone back every week. I've finally found a place where I can be myself and belong.

Gina was 17 when she wrote this story. After graduating from college, she became a tech writer and web developer. She is the founding editor of lifehacker.com

Carolina Moya

Too Shy to Say Hi

By Eugene Han

I'm sitting in the corner of a mostly gay café when I notice a cute guy sitting across from me. Hoping that he's glancing at me too, I look again. Our eyes meet, but I quickly turn away. I'm feeling nervous, so my stomach tightens. Still, I take a chance and look back.

He's still looking! Could he be interested? Taking his gaze as a sign, I walk over to sit next to him and say...

Well, that's when I get stuck, because in reality I'm still sitting in my chair, too shy to approach my admirer.

I've had a few experiences like that, too unsure of myself and afraid of rejection to make the first move. There are places where some gay guys will go up to other guys and ask them out immediately. Sometimes I wish I had the guts to do that.

My insecurities hinder my ability to approach guys.

Throughout my life, there have been people who said they would be there for me but then left. So it's hard for me to trust and reach out to people that I already know, much less strangers. I'm also insecure about my body and feel unattractive most of the time. I fear that if someone I approach rejects me, my looks would be the reason.

My insecurities hinder my ability to approach guys.

When I see someone I'm attracted to and I'm dealing with my anxieties, a series of thoughts rushes through my head. I ask myself: "What happens if he says yes? Will we hit it off as friends? If we start dating and it gets serious, will it last? Is he ready for an actual relationship, to deal with all that comes with it?"

After these initial questions, I begin to wonder if he's feeling and thinking the same things I am, especially since some gay guys haven't come to terms with their sexuality. I imagine drama, having to deal with the possibility of hiding our relationship from others, especially his parents. Or what if he's just sexually experimenting with men but is really straight? Then I would be left with the emotional aftermath of our break-up.

Even though some gays have a lot of issues, they seem to have no problem "hooking up." Still, according to what my friends say and from what I overhear at cafés and parties, a lot of these guys aren't interested in each other's feelings or trying to get to know each other. Instead, the hook-ups are mainly for fun, for a one-night stand.

I don't have a problem with others having casual sex, but I'm not looking for that. I hope to find a guy who's caring and who would stand by me through tough times. I want someone who wants to become close friends before anything serious begins, so that when there are hard times we would still have a bond that'll be hard to break.

Where would I find a guy like that? For now, I think my best bet is a local community center for gays and lesbians where I've made friends. I feel more comfortable striking up conversations there with people I don't know because the center has more of a group environment, with many familiar faces, and feels safer. Even though I haven't met anyone there who I'm interested in dating, I think I'll be more likely to ask someone out at the center when the chance comes along, than at a café or on the pier.

Still, I have a ways to go in overcoming my anxieties about asking guys out. I have to work on building my confidence about how I look and what I can offer a guy. I'm also trying to be more carefree and not overanalyze situations. I've talked about my feelings with my friends and they all say that I worry too much. They tell me that I should just enjoy the thrill of seeing a guy I'm attracted to and that there's little to be afraid about. If I get rejected when I ask someone out, it's simply his loss.

Of course, that's easy to say and much harder to experience. While being the aggressor is a fun idea, I hope other guys will find the courage to ask me out. That takes some pressure off me and shows that they're interested enough to take a risk. Then again, maybe they're as anxious as I am.

Eugene was 17 when he wrote this story.
He later attended college.

My Friend or My Church —How Do I Choose?

By Anonymous

I was talking on the phone with my friend Julian recently when he gave me a fright.

"Do you think I'm going to hell because I'm gay?" he asked.

We both go to Christian churches that consider homosexuality to be a sin. Right away I pictured him in hell surrounded by fire, getting tortured day in and day out. I tried to push the image away. I didn't want to think about my friend going to hell. Or dying, for that matter.

"I don't know. You should ask your pastor about that one, not me. I don't know what to tell you. Can we talk about something else?"

"Did I scare you?"

"Hell yeah, you scared me."

We started talking about something else, much to my relief. I felt really uncomfortable with his question because I didn't know the answer. My church says that being gay is a sin, so if

I follow my religion, yes, Julian is going to hell. But I know he isn't a bad person, and I don't think people choose to be gay. It's like a tug-of-war: my church pulling me by one arm and my gay friend pulling me by the other. I feel like my arms are about to be ripped off.

My religion is important to me because it's what holds me together. It makes me who I am. I get most of my values from the church. I've been a churchgoing girl my whole life. When I was little, I went to Pentecostal services with my grandmother. Then, eight years ago, our pastor started her own church, which began as Baptist but now isn't connected to any denomination.

So far in my life, what the church tells me to do and not to do has felt right to me—I don't drink, I don't smoke, I don't lie, and I try to treat other people with respect. I believe in God. No matter what kind of problems I have, I can put them in His hands. It's a relief to me. Even though I can't see Him physically, I know He's still there to help me.

And when people at church know I have a problem, they pray for me. I see my church as part of my family. We all know each other. There are about 60 of us, and every week we talk and laugh after services. We've taken trips together, and when my grandmother was in the hospital my pastor visited her every day.

The last time my pastor spoke about homosexuality in a sermon, she said, "Being gay is a sin and should be acknowledged as such."

I'm 16 now and until two years ago I agreed with her, just as I agreed with everything else my church taught me. I thought gay people were immoral.

My mom has lots of gay friends. (I live with my grandmother, not with my mother. But my mom lives nearby and I see her often. She doesn't go to church but she does believe in God.) Until I was 13 I didn't know her friends were gay, and when I found out I felt awkward having them around me. They'd come by the house once or twice a month and introduce themselves, but I didn't want anything to do with them.

Still, I had to be polite and act like I cared about what they had to say. My mom tried to talk to me about it. "I saw how you were acting around them," she told me. "Don't think I didn't notice." But I avoided the issue. I just didn't want to deal with it.

One day when I was 14, one of my mom's friends and I were in the living room, and he started talking to me about being gay and the kinds of things he has to put up with.

I don't think that being gay is completely right, but I don't think that it's completely wrong, either.

"We live in the type of world that, in a way, refuses to accept gay people," he said. "It can be hard living in a society where the people in it look at you as being gay instead of just being you."

Right away I felt guilty. Maybe I was acting the same way toward him and I didn't even realize it. We kept talking and he started giving me advice about college and careers. He was a good listener, the kind of laid-back person who makes jokes to make you feel comfortable. I realized that just because he likes men, it doesn't mean he's a bad person. Yet I still thought that being gay was wrong.

At the time, I didn't know my friend Julian was gay and I don't think he did, either. When Julian first started going to my middle school, a lot of people thought he was gay. His voice sounds a little bit like a girl's and he wears tight clothes. But he always said he wasn't gay and after a while people just dropped the subject.

I'd been friends with Julian since the middle of 7th grade. We hung out and talked on the phone three or four times a week. We teased each other all the time, like about grades. When I was slipping, he'd joke about beating me up if I didn't improve my grades. I'd say the same to him. Julian wasn't serious about everything. He knew how to have fun.

About a year after my conversation with my mom's friend, I saw Julian's number on my caller ID. I picked up, expecting him to greet me with a joke as usual.

"I have to tell you something about me," he said. As soon as he said that I got a little scared.

"What?"

"Promise me you won't go crazy."

"Promise! What, are you gay?"

Silence. Then he said, "Yeeaaahh."

I stayed silent for about two minutes. I didn't know what to say. "Have you lost your mind?" I thought. "Gay!? What you know about being gay? You're 15. What the hell are you thinkin', boy?"

Those were just some of the things I wanted to say to him. But I didn't say any of them because I knew it had taken a lot for him to call me. I didn't want to be hard on him. Instead, I told him I was surprised, even though part of me wasn't. We'd been friends for two years at this point.

Still, I kept thinking over and over, "Oh my God, I have a gay friend now." I thought maybe it was just a phase that would pass in a couple of weeks.

I knew I wanted to be a friend to Julian, no matter what his sexuality was. I thought about what my mom's friend had told me about how gays are treated. To me, when you choose to do something wrong, that's a sin. But if you don't have a choice, I'm not so sure.

As time passed it became obvious that Julian wasn't going through a phase. He really is attracted to men and I don't think he decided to be that way. Neither did two other friends of mine who have since told me they're gay. My friendship with all three of them hasn't changed a bit. Actually, it's kind of fun to tell a boy that you think another boy is cute and have him agree with you. But I also worry that Julian and my other friends will go to hell.

I'm confused as heck. I don't think that being gay is completely right, but I don't think that it's completely wrong, either. Yet, according to my church, I can't stay on both sides of the question. If I were to choose my church, then I'd go back to thinking that homosexuality is completely wrong. That would mean telling my friends that they need to change their lives or they're going to hell. They wouldn't change, of course, and then I'd have to stop hanging out with them. I don't think I want to do that. I don't want to lose old friends just because of my religion.

But if I decide that homosexuality is morally acceptable, then I wonder what other church teachings I'll disagree with. Maybe I'll start to question my church altogether. And the more I question my religion, the further I'll stray from it. I don't want to do that, because God and the people in my church have given me so much support.

I'm not ready to make my choice. For now, I'm going to keep going to church every week and I'm going to keep hanging out with my friends. I hate being stuck in the middle. I hate worrying that my friends are going to hell. I hate feeling like a hypocrite, but I want to make sure I make the right decision.

The author was in high school when she wrote this story.

Chris Pope / Gabriel Appleton

Gay on the Block

By Jeremiah Spears

Because I'm 6'6" and hefty, people often think I should be a ballplayer of some sort. But once you get to know me, you'll know I'm no ballplayer. In my old neighborhood, guys would always call me out of my house to play basketball, knowing that was not what I liked to do. When I missed a shot they would ridicule me and call me a faggot.

It's true, I'm gay, and though I look like your ordinary clean-cut boy, I act a little feminine. When I'm happy I like to buy shoes. I also like to read romances and family-oriented books. My favorite book is *Mama* by Terry McMillan. It's about a divorced black woman with five kids who's having problems being accepted into society.

In fact, I've been diffrent my whole life. I first realized I was homosexual at an early age, because when I was around 5 or 6 years old I would see boys and think, "How cute." Besides, I was labeled "different" by many people. I never liked to play ball or get sweaty. My favorite toy was Christmastime Barbie. When the boys used to roughhouse and try to get me to do it too, I'd tell them to leave me alone. I would never do anything that boys did, such as sports, play fighting, or rapping.

I could never understand why anyone would want to harass me for that. I used to think, "So what if I'm gay? So what if I'm different? Accept me or don't accept me at all, honey, because I'm just me." I couldn't understand why the boys wanted to bother me and fight me when they didn't know a damn thing about me. But they did.

I thought the world was so against me and that no one cared.

The boys in my neighborhood were ruffneck, ball-playing, weed-smoking boys who picked on people to prove their toughness to their friends. I think those boys did what they did because of their own insecurities, because they wanted to prove they were manly men. There were about nine or 10 of them and they lived in or around my neighborhood. Wherever I went I always ran into them, and often they would torture me for being gay.

One Halloween night, I went alone to catch the bus to go to a party. I was wearing a pair of dark jeans and a matching jacket and a black sweater with my initials on it. My mother had spent a lot for the outfit. While I was walking toward the bus, I saw a group of boys on bikes passing by. I recognized some of the guys. My first thought was, "Oh no, they're going to start trouble with me." I kept walking.

All of a sudden a bottle of urine hit me and got all over me. Some straight guys think doing something like that to a gay guy is kind of creative. They hurried away while I screamed and cried because of all the money my mom spent on the outfit.

Then I felt the same as always—puzzled as to why I had to be their victim. I thought these guys would never understand me. I felt like the things the boys said and did to me were marks for life.

For three weeks after Halloween, I had the incident on my mind. At first my brothers wanted to beat the boys up. But I thought it wouldn't make the situation better. It would probably just wild up the problem more. Finally I decided that I'd show them I wouldn't stand for it anymore and I began to fight—with my pen. I wrote them gruesome letters smeared with ketchup for fake blood to let them know I was going to get them back and that I'd get the last laugh. Ha!

Usually, when the guys harassed me, I would tell them, "Go straight to hell because I'm going to be me, and there will be no changes until I feel that my life needs a change." And I would get revenge. I would make fun of them trying to talk to girls and getting turned down. Then I would get physical with them.

When we fought, often my brothers or my girl friends would be there to help me—some of my girl friends were known for beating guys down. And once I even whacked a guy with a plank. While I was fighting, I'd think blood and more blood because of the traumatic experiences I'd been through. I wanted so much revenge on the boys who created trouble for me. Because of the fights, the cops were always at my house.

Even though it made me feel better for a short while to get revenge, I felt as if I was never going to succeed in having peace of mind. And after the fights were over, I didn't feel much better. Often I felt as if I never belonged and that no one would ever socialize with me because I was gay. I thought the world was so against me and that no one cared.

Still, there were people around who helped me and supported me, like my brothers and my friends. Looking back, I can see how much of a difference they made, even when times were at their hardest.

When I was living in my old neighborhood, my best friend was Lauryne. Beauty was her name, and we would go to the movies, the mall, or just hang in the park and talk about everything, from boys and love, to clothes, shoes, and jewelry.

Like a lot of my other girl friends, Lauryne didn't really care that I was gay. As a matter of fact, she praised me for having the nerve to be able to come out at an early age to my parents and siblings and not really worry about what they were going to think of me. She said things like, "You're brave," "You're courageous," and that she was lucky to have a friend like me.

It made me feel wonderful to know I had friends who honestly cared about me. It made me strong and gave me courage to be even more open about my sexuality, and to encourage other kids to come into the light and take the risks. It made me believe there would always be people to support me.

Another person who really helped me survive everything was my grandma, who raised me. From my grandma I learned strength, courage, patience, love, heartfulness, and to treat all people the same no matter what. My grandma taught me to learn new things from people who try to reach out and teach you. She taught me the golden rule: Do unto others as you want others to do unto you.

My grandma was born in 1919. She grew up on a farm and was born in a time when blacks weren't accepted and women weren't allowed to vote. My grandma saw so much—the Great Depression, prohibition, segregation, World War II, lynchings, civil rights. She would tell me about the marches, about the violence, and how once when she was in Jackson, Mississippi, she saw men cutting down two boys who had been lynched from a tree. She would tell me that life isn't that hard today, not after what she's seen and been through. She told me, "My dear, you haven't seen the harshness life can give you."

Sometimes people who have lived through hard times grow closed and mean and bigoted against people who are different from them. But my grandma had a strong sense of herself, and that made her open-minded to different things in life. She always said, "People must know themselves before they try to learn from another person," and that's exactly what she did.

My grandmother never tried to change me. Instead, she encouraged me to do what I thought was right and what would make me happy. My grandma often told me I would be different as time went on and that she'd always love me however I was.

One day I received a call from my aunt saying my grandma wanted to speak to me. When she got on the phone, she said, "I love you dear, and don't let no one turn you around." Then my grandma hung up the phone because she had gotten

The people who supported me made me feel that I didn't have to change myself for anyone.

short-winded. Shortly after that conversation, she died. I love her dearly and I miss her.

I no longer live in my old neighborhood and the boys no longer bother me because I don't go around there very often. When I think back on those times, sometimes I can laugh, but other times I'm still angry that those nobodies had so much control over my life. Still, I'm OK with being myself every day. Despite all the hassles I went through, the people who supported me made me feel that I didn't have to change myself for anyone. My life would only get harder if I tried to satisfy other people. I just need to satisfy myself.

Jeremiah was 18 when he wrote this story.
He now lives in Mississippi.

Mom, Dad, I Have Something to Tell You...

By José Miguel Jimenez

When I realized that I was gay, I knew that I couldn't tell everyone my self-discovery. If I did, I might face serious consequences, like getting homophobic comments hurled at me and getting into fistfights. But I didn't want to keep my revelation all to myself either. I wanted to share my enlightenment with some of my friends and teachers. And I wanted to eventually tell my parents. I didn't want there to be any big secrets between us.

Yet I didn't feel like I could tell them right away. Though I'd never heard them make homophobic comments, I didn't know how they'd handle my sexuality. I didn't expect anything too bad from my mother, since she's a lot more modern than my father.

He's tough and can be really old-fashioned about how things should be done in the house, how children should behave, and how to discipline them. My father is quicker to argue and fight than talk things out with his kids. I thought he'd get angry with me for being gay. I didn't think he'd approve of guys liking other guys.

So instead of telling my parents, I selectively told people I felt I could trust and who would accept me. Telling them was like setting up a safety net for when I chose to tell my parents—I'd be able to turn to them for support if my parents rejected me.

I decided to tell my friends Oscarina, Vanessa, and Belinda first. I knew that they'd be OK with it. Vanessa had helped me realize that I was gay, and Oscarina had told me before that she didn't have a problem with gay people. I knew Belinda would be surprised by the news, which she was, but she dealt with it well.

My English teacher, Ms. Somerville, was the first adult I decided to tell. We'd talked before about what was going on in my life. She was also in charge of the poetry club, where I got to see her as more as a friend than as just a teacher. A few days after figuring out that I was gay, I waited to talk to her after class.

"I'm gay," I blurted out, looking away for a fraction of a second.

"That's great," she said, smiling and giving me a hug. She said it was perfectly normal. She immediately made me feel more confident about who I am.

It felt great to be supported, but I still didn't feel up to telling my parents. After some careful thought I decided to tell my sister Katherine, who's a year older than me. We'd grown close since we were kids, and I occasionally confided in her about my life. My sister has adopted a lot of my parents' viewpoints, so I figured telling her would be a good way to measure how they might react.

"I'm gay," I said one morning in our bathroom as Katherine used the mouthwash. I got extremely anxious as I waited for a response.

"Hmmm."

Silence.

"I'm not surprised," she finally said after a few seconds. She said she thought I might be and that it was fine. I told her my concerns about our father and she agreed that I should hold off on telling him.

It was a relief to have told someone in my family. There was one less person I had to keep a big secret from. Maybe I'd even be able to talk to her about guys.

I was slowly gaining more confidence about telling my parents. But I was still very worried about how my father would react. So I decided to tell my Aunt Maritza. She's open-minded, and I trusted her to tell my parents for me in a sympathetic way.

When I told her she smiled. She said that she already knew and would handle telling my parents. But this didn't fully solve my problems. While my aunt did indeed tell my parents, I knew that they wouldn't talk about my sexuality with me unless I brought it up first.

I wanted everything to be openly discussed between us, so there wouldn't be any tension. I wanted to be honest about the things I was doing, like working with a gay-related organization.

I chose to speak to my mother first. One day we sat on her bed to talk. I was beating around the subject of my sexuality throughout the entire conversation.

"If you're going to say it, then just say it," she suddenly said. So I told her and she said she wasn't too surprised. I felt relaxed now that I'd told one of my parents. But then she said she wanted me to tell my father.

"You've got to be kidding," I said.

"It won't be as bad as you think," she replied.

I wanted to avoid a hostile confrontation, but my mother insisted.

I held back. But a few days later, while I was getting ready for summer school, I walked into my parents' room to get some lotion. My mother was sitting on their bed. My father was ironing a shirt.

"Tell him," my mother said. I looked at her, surprised and annoyed that she chose this moment to have me do it. I had to leave for school in a few minutes.

"Tell him," she repeated.

I turned to my father, wishing that I could hide. He looked at me expectantly. It didn't seem to matter that he already knew.

I have to tell you something," I said.

"What? You have a girl-friend?" he said jokingly.

I watched my father's face closely, waiting for an explosion.

"No, I don't," I answered, only half looking at him. "And you know that I'm not going to have one."

His face grew very serious. I was tense. Time stopped. I thought that I would be stuck forever in that moment, stuck with that feeling of dread. I watched his face closely, waiting for an explosion. Was this the calm before the storm?

But he didn't freak out. We talked for the next five minutes. He was calm and didn't say anything about how it was bad to be gay. He told me how I had to be careful, that there are not only people who wouldn't accept me, but diseases like HIV/AIDS.

I nodded that I already knew all this because I wanted the conversation to end as quickly as possible. Now that I'd spoken to him about it, I didn't want to talk about it anymore. All my feelings about being open had flown away. It felt too weird talking to him about my gayness.

My mother dismissed me, saying that I needed to leave or I'd be late for school. I left happy, knowing that everything had been cleared. I think that my father was so calm because he'd talked to my aunt. He had time to digest the news.

But despite what I'd hoped for, things are far from open in my house. I only talk to my sister Katherine about being gay. It feels too odd to talk about guys with my parents, particularly since my father can be so overprotective. I went to a park the other day just to chill. Because he'd heard that gay men have sex there, he freaked out and started lecturing me. At times like these, I try to zone him out. While he may be trying to protect me, it also shows how he has a lot to learn about me since I don't do sex in parks.

Coming out to my parents was one of the most difficult experiences in my life, but that was partially because I'd expected the worst. I'm pleased with how I went about telling them and thankful I had the support of other people. Still, I'm glad that it's over, and hope I never have to go through something like that again.

José Miguel Jimenez graduated from SUNY-Purchase College in New York.

Gabriel Appleton

Trapped!

By Mariah Lopez

Being transgendered isn't easy, especially when you're living in a straight group home and you're the only one. But first, let me tell you what a transgender is. Yeah, I know, the first thing that pops into your head is a man with a sex change and a dress. Wrong! A transgender is someone who lives his or her life as the opposite sex. It doesn't mean that they have a sex change (that's a transsexual).

I'm a guy but I've felt like a female my whole life. And when I dress the part, I look a lot like a female, too. I can even get numbers from guys. (But I always tell them right then and there that I'm a guy.)

I know a lot of people are uncomfortable with who I am, but I hope the fact that I'm transgendered doesn't stop you from reading more. After all, you're learning, aren't you? So let me continue. I'm 14 years old. When I was six, my grandmother (who raised me) told me I was a boy. Until then, I didn't know that. I felt and thought like a girl. I walked with my chest sticking out and I liked to wear my hair in a pony tail. I even liked dressing in girls' clothes.

When I was growing up everyone knew me and my family, so they didn't bother me. But when I went into foster care at the age of 8, it was a different story.

The first group home I was in, where I stayed for three years, was terrible. So were a lot of other group homes I've been in. But they weren't terrible at first, because my grandmother was still alive and when anything happened to me, she would report the staff to the social worker and complain.

But after she passed, things got worse and worse. I had at least two fights a day. The boys used to do stupid things because I was gay, like throw rocks at me or put bleach in my food. Once I was thrown down a flight of stairs and I've had my nose broken twice. They even ripped up the only picture of my mother that I had.

Often the staff were bad, too. If I had a fight with one of the staff earlier in the day, they would start conversations with the other boys in the group home about the argument just to get them riled up. Then the boys would come up to me, challenging me and calling me a faggot. Sometimes the staff would stand there while the kids jumped me. One time a staff member jumped me with the kids.

My grandmother always told me to be myself and be proud. But when these things were happening I didn't know what to do or who to turn to. Most of the time the staff told me the same things.

"You deserve it."

"Oh well."

"Fight back."

"Don't be gay then."

One time a staff member asked me, "Don't you like men beating on you?" Another staff even told me to kill myself to be out of my misery.

When I got to go to my room, I'd just sit there and cry. Or I'd read a book or listen to music to block things out of my head. I slept a lot, too, so that the days would go by faster. I used to get mad and think, "What's so bad about me?" I'd pray and ask God why He didn't make me a girl or a straight boy so I wouldn't have to go through this. Sometimes I would cry all night, asking Him to change me.

But I never really felt I could change. I was who I was and couldn't change that.

The boys would come up to me, challenging me and calling me a faggot.

Through all of these things, I had one constant feeling—the feeling of helplessness, that no matter what I did or didn't do, it would always be the same and that somehow it was all my fault.

I stayed at my first group home for three years. Then one day I went AWOL with only three dollars in my pocket and nothing to lose. I just decided that I had to get off that campus. When I got to the train, I talked the conductor into letting me ride for free. And when I arrived in the city, let me tell you, I hadn't been so happy since I don't know when.

I tried to stay at Green Chimneys, a group home for gay and transgendered boys. But they didn't have room for me and I was too young. Eventually I went back into the foster care system. For the next year I bounced around from group home to group home. I always left because being transgendered was always a problem. I knew I'd be bouncing around until I could get into Green Chimneys or until someone opened another group home for gay kids.

There were a few staff and kids who made me feel really good about myself. At one group home the staff taught the kids that they should respect me, and that helped the kids to be more open-minded. I was even able to date openly. But in most of the group homes people constantly harassed me. After about a year I finally got a phone call from my law guardian telling me that I had a bed at Green Chimneys, so I packed my bags.

When I got there, I still couldn't believe it. I finally felt content—that I could be myself and unique at the same time.

Sure, there are plenty of things that get me plucked (mad) at Green Chimneys. Just living with a bunch of other teens in foster care can be a nightmare (not that I'm always such a little sweetheart myself). But if it weren't for a supportive group home, I'd still be in a very uncomfortable position and so would a whole lot of other kids.

Mariah was 14 when s/he wrote this story. She has done outreach work related to AIDS/HIV, and is an activist and advocate for queer youth of color in foster care.

Qing Zhuang

Date With Destiny

By Anonymous

(All names in this story have been changed.)

Let me tell you about the day that changed my destiny. It was July 30, 10 days after I turned 20 years old. I was working for a health agency and living in an apartment in New York. I was excited about being on my own. Little did I know how my life was going to change on this day.

Let's backtrack a little. Two weeks before, I had gotten tested for HIV. I began to get tested when I was 16 years old because I was engaging in sex and sometimes I didn't use a condom. I wanted to be sure that I hadn't gotten infected.

It wasn't a big deal because I had gotten tested many times before and always got a negative result, meaning I didn't have HIV. And since my last test, the only time I'd had sex without a condom with was someone I'd been in a long-term relationship with. He assured me that he had been tested for HIV and that he did not have it. And even though he refused to show me the test results, I trusted him, so I believed him. He had been asking me to have unprotected sex for some time, and I eventually gave in. The condoms went out the window for the duration of our relationship.

After about a year and a half, our relationship ended. He had become way too controlling for me. I wasn't allowed to go out with my friends or do the things I used to do before I met him. The last straw for me was when he told me that he needed to "mold" me into the person he wanted me to be. I told him to get some clay and mold his next boyfriend. I walked out and that was that. It wasn't long before I was over him and loving being single.

So back to July 30. It was a hot summer day. I went to work as usual. Nothing was different except for me having to get back my HIV results. I had taken the test in the HIV testing center of the agency where I worked. When it was time to go see what my results were, I said a prayer and ran down the two flights of stairs to the sixth floor.

The receptionist told me to have a seat and someone would be with me. I sat and began to thumb through a magazine. I didn't read any of the articles, because though I wasn't really worried, I always felt a little anxiety wondering what the results of my HIV test would be. I began to recall the times that I had not practiced safe sex in my life. Then I reminded myself that I had only done that with people who I knew were HIV negative. After all, I had asked them.

Excuse me, Pedro?" a voice called out, interrupting my thoughts.

It was the director of the department. It was agency policy for employees to the see the director for test results. She was a very pleasant woman who could have you feeling like her best friend within the first few minutes of meeting her.

I stood and shook her hand. "Let's go into my office so we can have a little more privacy," she said. I followed her into the office and we made small talk. She opened a drawer and took out a file.

She began to go over the routine stuff, telling me what the three possible test results were, the stuff you hear every time you get tested for HIV. It was either: an HIV negative result, meaning I didn't have HIV; an HIV inconclusive result, meaning the test was unable tell whether I had HIV, and I would need to be tested again; or an HIV positive result, meaning I had somehow contracted HIV.

As she went on, I got more and more anxious. I just wanted to know what the results were. After all, I'd heard this stuff a million times before.

I always felt a little anxiety wondering what the results of my HIV test would be.

Soon she was telling me what I would need to do if I was negative. "Be sure to continue practicing safe sex, get tested in six months, and be with only one partner," she said, sounding like a mother telling me to wear clean socks.

Then she started talking about what I would need to do if I tested positive for HIV. I tuned her out then because I didn't want to think about what it would be like and how my life would change if I did have HIV.

"OK, and now for your results," she said.

"Ladies and gentlemen, the envelope please," I thought to myself.

She opened the file and placed it on her desk. As always, I was officially nervous. No matter how many times I'd done this before, I couldn't help but feel anxious those last few minutes right before I found out if my life was going to change or stay the same.

"Pedro, your results came back positive," she blurted.

The blood ran from my body. A wave of nerves washed over me. I needed to breathe. I was in shock. How? Why? But most of all, who? Who gave me HIV?

I swallowed and tried to compose myself. I kept telling myself to breathe. Why me? I was so young. After breaking up with my boyfriend, I was looking forward to a new life, a second chance at living again. I was wrecked. I felt as if I had let down people who cared about me. I felt guilty for being gay. I felt like this was a punishment from God. I did everything possible to prevent myself from crying.

"Are you OK?" she was asking.

"Yeah, fine." It was a lie, of course.

"I think it may be a good idea if you take the rest of the day off. If you have the time, you might want to take a few days off to relax and absorb this. This is not going to be easy for you, but you can do it. Understand that this does not mean a death sentence."

She started explaining that the results were not going to be shown to anyone without my permission. Everything else she said was just a blur. I couldn't listen anymore. I needed to leave. I wanted to go home and crawl up in bed. I didn't want to think about this. Not now.

I went straight to my boss's office. I told her what had happened and that I needed to leave immediately. She was understanding, and allowed me to take off the next two days. I went outside and walked around aimlessly for two hours.

I was angry, so angry. I didn't know what to do with myself so I tried calling my ex to tell him what had happened. I was confident that he was the one who infected me. He was the only one who I had been with for over a year and a half. I finally reached him and told him about the test. To add insult to injury, he was more concerned about who I had told than how I was doing. He didn't want any of my friends getting revenge on him.

I told him I was on my way over. By the time I got to his house, I was fuming mad. I wanted answers and I wanted them yesterday.

"How could you do this to me?" I asked.

"Who did you tell?" he still wanted to know.

"What does it matter? I told those who are concerned about me."

"You shouldn't have done that. Why didn't you call me first? We could have handled this together."

"No, we couldn't have," I replied, getting more agitated by the moment. "Look, all I want to know is, are you positive?"

"Uh, yeah, I just got tested recently and I found out I was positive."

"You what?" My voice was getting louder and I was beginning to get choked up. I couldn't

I needed to breathe. I was in shock. How? Why? But most of all, who? Who gave me HIV?

believe this was happening. "I think you are lying and I also think that you've been positive longer than you say you have. How could you do this? I asked you over and over if you were negative and you lied to me! What am I supposed to do now?"

"Listen, baby, we can work this out." He tried to pull me closer to him.

"Get off of me! There is nothing to work out!" I pulled away from him. I had heard enough. I wanted to get out. "Damn you! Don't ever bother me again!" I screamed. I was crying now. There was nothing more to say or do. I picked up my book bag, wiped my face with my shirt and stormed out of his house. My head was pounding. I could hear him calling me to come back. I kept walking.

I went home and got in bed. I couldn't eat. I felt as if my life had stopped. I had so many emotions swirling in my head that I could not even think straight.

As I lay in my bed, I remembered all the people I already

knew who were living with HIV. They were able to do everything they wanted to do in their lives. Nothing stopped them. Their sense of humor about it also helped them to deal with it better. Remembering them made me feel a little calmer.

I knew I could talk to them about what I was going through. I also knew I had many other people who could help support me. I kept telling myself that I was fortunate to have tested positive now and not in 1988, a time when little was known about HIV and there were very few medications available.

But I was also pissed off. Although the responsibility of deciding to have unsafe sex fell in my lap, I was angry because I had given my ex the benefit of the doubt. I had trusted him. And he had failed me. I felt like he took my life away from me.

I wanted to get even with him for lying to me. But deep inside, I knew that revenge would get me nowhere. Even after I did get my revenge, I would still be HIV positive. Nothing could change that. Not now.

I fell asleep hoping that when I awoke, this day would have been a dream.

After several weeks, once the initial shock of learning that I was positive wore off, I began looking for ways that I could improve my life, both physically and emotionally. I'd never allowed any challenge in my life to take me down before and I was not about to let this one be the first.

I began to go to therapy to help myself deal with being HIV positive. Therapy taught me that although I may be faced with a life-threatening illness, I shouldn't use it as a reason for not trying to achieve the things I want in life. In fact, it should be the reason for achieving the goals I want, such as finishing college and moving out of New York. Therapy also helped me accept that being positive was not a punishment from God for being gay. My therapist told me, "God doesn't give nothing you can't handle." It was then that I promised myself that I would not give up without a fight.

I started spending a lot of time alone, just looking at my life. If I wanted to live longer, I knew that I needed to spend more time on me and less time in the clubs. I needed to make sure that I got enough rest, reduced my stress and took my medications.

Above all, though, I needed to practice safe sex at all times. I did not want to infect another person. I did not want to live the rest of my days knowing that I was responsible for that.

I went back to college soon after finding out that I was HIV positive. I wrote a final report, which was close to 175 pages, about learning to cope with HIV. Part of the final report required me to do journal entries to help me deal with the feelings I was having around being positive. Writing the paper and those journal entries really helped me put what happened to me over the past year into perspective. It helped me realize how strong a person I really was. It also helped me find ways of coping, such as exercising, talking more with my friends, and taking acupuncture when life was getting too stressful for me.

I got an A+ on the paper and was the only student in my class to make it onto the dean's list that semester.

This past summer marked three years since I learned that I was positive. I am now working as the administrative director for a community foundation, and am still trying to finish that college degree. My viral load is undetectable, which means that the amount of HIV in my body is so low that the current available tests cannot detect it. It does not mean that I am negative, it just means that there isn't a lot of HIV in my system. This is due, in part, to me taking my medications and living a healthier life.

More important, I have gradually managed to come to terms with my HIV status. I've learned to forgive myself for being HIV positive. I don't consider this a punishment from God. I consider it sort of like a tap on the shoulder telling me that I need to take better care of myself and not be so reckless with my life because I only have one shot at living.

Believe it or not, I also forgave the person who infected me.

I had the opportunity to protect myself and I chose not to. I can live with that. Being angry at him or trying to be vengeful towards him will not make the HIV leave my body. I want to live a happy life, not a bitter one. Although he is no longer in my life, I know that I would be able to see him in the street and not want to get into a fist fight with him.

One of the major concerns I had when I became infected was whether I would be able to find a new boyfriend who would love and accept me even though I had HIV. Thankfully, I have been blessed with a boyfriend who does. When he and I first met, I was scared to tell him because I did not want to be rejected. But I wanted to tell him because I did not want to mislead him. When I did tell him, I was surprised by his reaction. Not only did he say that he was cool with it, but he also told me that he was very happy that I'd told him. We have now been together a year and three months and we are living together. Yes, you can say happily ever after.

I have learned to be grateful for what I have now that I'm living with HIV. The expensive medications I need are covered by my health insurance. There are so many in this world who don't even know they have HIV, or don't have access to the costly care they need. Even though I have an illness that is fatal, I am better off than a lot of people. I can see, walk, and talk. I am able to work and provide for myself. By taking a step back and counting my blessings, I have been able to see that I am not that bad off.

I am looking forward to living a healthy, long life. My doctor tells me that if I take my medications and follow his orders, he can help me live to the age of 60. I am confident that this will happen. And with all the research going on about HIV, maybe, just maybe, they might come up with a cure.

The author graduated from college and lives and works in New York City.

Karolina Zaniesienko

I Need a Girl

By Destiny Cox

I was a 13-year-old high school freshman when I realized that I was attracted to females. I felt funny because I didn't know anyone who was a lesbian. I didn't understand why I was feeling this way, so I wasn't comfortable with my attraction. I didn't want to face that I was seriously looking at girls like a guy would.

I didn't think I could reveal my attractions to any of my friends, because, for us, it was about how to get boys to like you. I'd had "boyfriends" and had even kissed a boy. So I convinced myself that I was merely curious about being with the same sex.

But one girl brought a major change to how I looked at my sexuality. She lived near my house. I usually saw her around, often by the neighborhood church. But I didn't know her name. Every time I saw her, I stared and got nervous and clumsy. My heart beat like a drum and my chest got tight. I even tripped on the curb once while looking at her walk.

One day I was with my friend Susan and we saw her again.

"Hi, Keesha," Susan said.

"Wassup, girl," Keesha replied. Susan introduced me to Keesha, and we said right there that we should hang out since we saw each other so often. I started to spend a lot of time with Keesha on the weekends and saw her after school sometimes. We were the same age and both liked to watch horror movies and write. Sometimes we acted out our stories at home. And when we went shopping together, we bought each other gifts.

Spending time with Keesha made me like her a lot more. About two months after we were introduced, I decided that I had to tell her how I felt. I knew it was risky, but I couldn't hold it in any longer. I was scared that my feelings for her would get too intense if I continued to hold them in.

We were at her house one day, and I knew I had to tell her then and there. My palms were sweating and my head started to itch. I had no idea what she'd tell me after I told her. Keesha had accepted that her mother is bisexual and that her best friend, Michael, is gay. Still, I didn't know how she felt about a girl having feelings for her.

So, as we were gossiping, I came out and said, "I have to tell you something."

"What?" she replied.

I stalled, and then said, "Well, before I met you, I used to see you all the time."

"You used to look at me mad funny," she said.

"Well...I was just looking because I was attracted to you," I said timidly.

Keesha looked very surprised. Then she blushed. "Well," she said. "I like you too."

This could not be real. I kept on asking her if she was serious. Although she kept saying yes, it didn't hit me until she kissed me on my lips. I'd never kissed a girl before.

When I'd kissed a boy, I felt nothing. When I kissed Keesha, I felt butterflies in my stomach. Her lips felt like rose petals and tasted like orange lip-gloss.

After we got over the initial shock of our attraction to each other, Keesha and I became a couple. But we never showed it in public; we always made sure that whoever saw us thought of us as friends. We didn't want to be criticized by other people, so we told no one about our romance.

What mattered more to me was that Keesha was in my life. I cared for Keesha a lot and hugged her tight every time we met. I wrote her letters almost every day. We spent hours talking to each other on the phone and instant messaging each other on the computer.

When I kissed Keesha, I felt butterflies in my stomach.

About a month and a half into our relationship, she told me she loved me. And I loved her too. My time with Keesha made me realize how happy I could be dating a girl. I loved it. Before meeting her, I daydreamed about being with a girl and being happy, and being with Keesha was even better than I'd hoped.

Unfortunately, my relationship with Keesha started to change about a week after we revealed our love to each other. I started going to dance practice on Saturdays and after-school classes, so I saw her less. She started to put on a musical for her school and to sing in the talent show. We stopped having time for each other.

One night on the phone, I told Keesha we were drifting apart. I said we should just be friends. She sounded sad. I felt sad too. I cried after I hung up because I didn't want her to hear me cry and then start crying too. It was hard, but I felt it was for the best. My relationship with Keesha lasted three months. Thankfully, we're still friends.

Soon after being with her, I made up my mind that I was a lesbian and that I didn't want to be with guys anymore. The strong love and attraction I felt for Keesha was what I knew I could feel for another girl, not a guy.

Three months after breaking up with Keesha, I started to tell some of my friends I was a lesbian because I felt comfortable enough with my sexuality to risk coming out. I also told my parents.

I'm 16 now and have dated other girls since Keesha. Some of those relationships have been even better than when I dated her because they were out in the open. I have a girlfriend now. I can hold her hand in public and not care about the eyes that I know are looking at us. I can kiss her in public without looking over my shoulder to check if I see anyone I know. My relationship with Keesha helped me get to this point. She was my first girlfriend, and I'll never forget her.

After graduating from high school, Destiny attended Delaware State University and joined the Navy. She is currently stationed in Japan.

Karolina Zaniesienko

Telling My Parents

By Destiny Cox

"Why are all these dykey girls calling the house?" my mother asked me one day, referring to some of my female friends. "Why do you stay on the phone with girls for hours?" I always found a way to dodge the questions.

When I was 13, I began to realize that I was a lesbian. Over time, I made lesbian friends and dated different girls. But I was scared to tell my parents. Still, mom saw that something was up.

I was close to both my mom and dad. Still, I felt closer to dad, even though we didn't live together. My father's a funny guy. I talked to him mostly about school, video games, and the people who got on my nerves. I spoke to mom about school a lot, too. I usually asked her for help with my homework.

I felt loved by my parents and liked to talk about my future with them. Dad said that he wanted me to become a famous writer. My mother said she wanted me to be rich and successful. She also wanted me to have a husband and kids. My brother, who passed away, had one son, who my mom rarely sees. She said I was her only hope for more grandkids.

My parents thought there was nothing major to worry about with me, and so I felt like I had their full support. That changed when I realized I liked girls. I felt weird since I was brought up believing that humans should be with the opposite sex. I wanted to talk to my mother and father about my attraction, but knew it would cause controversy.

I'd overheard my mother talking to her friends about how homosexuals were messing up the human reproduction cycle. And my father felt comfortable calling feminine guys "faggots." I wasn't sure how he'd react to having a lesbian daughter.

I eventually met a girl, Keesha, who became my first girl-friend. [See my other story on p. 71.] I wanted to tell my parents about her because I loved her, but I wasn't ready.

Being with Keesha helped me feel better about my sexual-ity. A month after we broke up, I started dating other girls on the down low and made lesbian friends. I often took pictures with them.

When my mother saw my pictures, she noticed some of the girls dressed in a masculine style. She asked me if they were les-bians. I told her they were tomboys. Questions like that brought fear to my heart. I thought if I told her I was a lesbian, she'd tell me to live with my father because of how much she disliked homosexuality.

But I was also tired of keeping a big part of my life secret. I felt bad lying. I was scared to come out to her, but still wanted to give her a hint. So I started to wear rainbow colors, which are a symbol of gay pride, on my wrist and neck.

Three weeks later I was sitting in my room reading when mom asked me straight out, "Destiny, are you a lesbian?" She'd noticed the rainbow jewelry and knew what it stood for.

Scared to death, I asked her, "Why would you say something like that?"

"Just answer the question," she said.

I didn't know whether to lie or tell the truth. I felt very, very scared. I thought that I might as well tell her the truth now, because if she found out later she'd be more upset.

"Yes, I am."

She laughed in my face and said that it was a phase. I think she was in denial. Still, at that moment, I hoped she'd leave me alone and let me go through my "phase."

> Mom asked me straight out, 'Destiny, are you a lesbian?'

The day after I told my mother, I went to tell dad because I knew she'd eventually tell him. While walking up the stairs to his house, I had the same nervous feeling I had when I told my mom.

"What do you have to talk to me about?" he asked.

"Well, daddy, I want you to know that I'm different."

"What do you mean?"

"Well, I like girls," I said, feeling better that I got it out.

"How?" he said, looking at me funny.

"I have the same feelings toward girls as you do," I said.

He looked at me with a comical, surprised face. "Whatever. You're going through a phase, little girl."

"No, I am not!" I yelled. I didn't want him to think it was a phase too. Knowing my father, he'd start joking about it. He saw in my eyes that I was serious.

"What you're doing is not right," he said. "I can't accept it. But you're going to do what you want to do anyway, so I can't stop you. But I do love you, princess."

"I know, daddy," I said.

"You can talk to me about it more if you want," he said.

"No, that's OK," I said. I wanted to leave because I didn't want to look at him, knowing he knew about me. I felt that if I stayed, he'd ask me questions I didn't feel like answering.

I went home and sat by myself. Knowing that both of my parents knew about my sexuality made me feel more free. I also felt OK about dad's response, because even though he said something negative about my preference, he also said something positive.

Being around my mother was hell, though, because I didn't know when she'd start talking about it. I just wasn't comfortable talking about my sexuality with her knowing that she was so against it. So I tried to stay in my room. But mom didn't say anything about my sexuality, so I slowly started to feel more comfortable around her. I figured she was getting over her shock.

Two weeks after coming out to her, I started to let my lesbian friends hang out at my house. My mother didn't say anything at first. Then one day, she suddenly told me that I couldn't bring home any girls who looked like boys. She said that bringing butch dykes to the house was a dead giveaway to neighbors who I thought I was a lesbian.

I followed her rules but I was hurt, because I felt like she was ashamed of me. She was being immature and prejudiced.

It's been a year since I came out to her, and she still thinks I'll soon be straight. She sometimes asks me if I've met any new girls, just to be sarcastic. If I need to talk to her about how I'm feeling about a girl, I know she'll criticize me, and I shouldn't have to feel that way. I want to talk to her about my relationships because she's my mother. I want to have that type of bond with her.

I don't talk to dad about my sexuality either because I still don't feel comfortable going there with him. I'm concerned he'll make offensive jokes about my sexuality.

Despite not wanting the neighbors to know about my sexuality, my mother still told other family members. Those who know also don't talk about it, except my cousin Jennifer, who's my age and straight. One day we were sitting in my room and she asked me, "Are you going to be this way forever?"

I told her that I couldn't predict my future, but I felt like I wanted to spend my life with a woman. She looked at me and said, "Destiny, that is you and I am not knocking it."

Jennifer's very sweet; I've always found her easy to talk to. When we talk about our relationships, Jennifer listens to what I say and I listen to her. I consider her more like a sister. She's shown me that family can respect me for who I am. I wish more of my family could be as open as she is.

My mother still thinks I'll soon be straight.

My friends, gay and straight, support me too. My two best friends come to my house and hang with mom and me all the time. They tell me that mom only wants the best for me, and that she and dad will come around.

I think my parents will support my sexuality one day, but not like Jennifer and my friends have. Still, when my parents are ready to deal with it, I'll be happier, because I know how great it will feel to be supported by them.

Jolie Prom

My Crushing Secret

By Anonymous

I first saw Miguel early sophomore year. It was 6th period and I'd gone to the main office where there was a candy drive. As I opened the door I saw him standing there, wearing blue jeans and a dark blue shirt and buying a Midnight Milky Way bar. He was about 5'9", with dark healthy-looking skin and very handsome. I could tell just by looking at him that he worked out.

And I couldn't stop looking at him. Time seemed to stand still. My mind went blank and I just stared at him, like "duh."

Then I snapped out of it and went about my business. I was embarrassed that I could be affected so strongly by this guy I didn't even know. I tried to push my thoughts of him back into my mind. That worked until I saw him in the hallway a few days later.

I became so infatuated with Miguel it wasn't funny. Almost every chance I got, during lunch or between classes, I roamed the halls hoping I would see him. He had such a powerful effect on me. If I was feeling crappy and saw him, I would immediately feel happy. Eventually I overheard one of his friends say his name in passing, and I learned that he was a senior.

I guess it's not uncommon for people to get big crushes on people they barely know, but in my case it was even more awkward because I was a guy practically in love with another guy.

I 'd never felt that way about a guy before. I wanted to know what was wrong with me that I couldn't control my emotions or feelings towards him. I couldn't understand it and I didn't know what to do. For the first time, I was truly afraid of something.

I had assumed automatically that I was straight. In 6th grade I had my first crush, on a girl named Maria. I wasn't nervous around her. I just thought she was pretty and nice. She was easy to talk to and we became friends. Now that I look back, though, there was this one guy in junior high I'd been attracted to. But he was always surrounded by pretty girls and I just assumed I was attracted to them or wished I was in that crowd.

And sophomore year, there was a guy named Johnny in my first period class that I liked. But my feelings for him were on a different level than my out-of-control feelings for Miguel. Johnny was handsome and friendly, but he didn't have the same impact on me.

I couldn't stop thinking about Miguel but, at the same time, I didn't want to think about my attraction to him. I didn't want to deal with what it might mean about my sexuality. Still, the subject kept popping up like an annoying ad on the internet. Did my crush on Miguel mean I was gay?

At the time I thought all gay people were sick, freaky-looking, smart, rich, and going to hell. These beliefs were a combination of what I picked up from my parents and the media. From movies and TV shows I got the idea that gay men had good paying jobs, but also dangerous lifestyles of drinking, drugs, and promiscuity.

Meanwhile, my parents believed that homosexuality was a

big sin, pure and simple. When issues like gay marriage or gay adoption came up on the news, they said things like, "That's nasty and disgusting." They told me stories about how "back in our day," gay people would stay in their houses and wait for death. I imagined them locked in their parents' basements or something. I knew if I told my parents I might be gay, I should have funeral arrangements ready. So I kept my crush a closely guarded secret.

I was terrified. It was like walking through a minefield. I hated it so much and felt horribly alone. But I couldn't see telling friends about my crush, either. Sometimes they'd claim to be fearful of gay people. Even if I changed the story a little by telling them it was an older girl I had the crush on, I knew they'd keep pestering me to tell who it was. Or worse, they'd pressure me to spill my guts to my crush.

In junior high school some friends had asked me plainly, "Are you gay?" I'd always say no, because in my mind at the time I was straight. Their asking didn't bother me, because I knew I did things in a unique manner. I was probably the only person they'd met aside from teachers who didn't curse every other word. And I had my own style of dressing—a little gothic, a little punk. But my classmates accepted me anyway.

Being a little different was all right, but my crush made me feel so weird. I felt possessed. It was like I was someone else when Miguel was around.

I'd fantasize about approaching him, but then I'd think, "How is he going to react? What would happen if someone else heard? What if he's flattered, but taken? What if he's a bonehead jock, and I put myself in a dangerous position?" Coming out to a stranger was something I wasn't ready to do. (I wasn't ready to come out to myself.) But I never saw him long enough to start a conversation with him, and I didn't know what I would say anyway.

Then one day, a few months after my first sighting, I had pool gym. Miguel emerged from the water looking so beautiful, like one of those Greek gods, with drops trickling down his skin. I was so excited I thought for sure I'd have a heart attack. I just sat there on the side of the pool looking at him, occasionally checking to see if other people were looking at me looking at him. I was afraid of what people might say if they saw me staring at him the way I was.

Even worse, I was "physically happy," but I was holding my coat in front of me, so that took care of that. It was a supremely embarrassing moment, but for the rest of day I held Miguel's image in my mind and a happy look on my face.

But I saw Miguel rarely after that. By the time he graduated in June, I was feeling less obsessed. I guess not seeing him cooled me off. Still, I wasn't completely over him. He was still in my thoughts and dreams.

I t wasn't until two years later when I was a senior that I told someone about him. I couldn't keep it in any more. I finally spilled the truth to a teacher I was close to. We'd talked before about other issues I'd had. He'd listened and been supportive and I felt I could trust him with my secret.

I felt like I was telling someone I was a secret agent for a foreign agency. But his attitude was, "Oh, OK, whatever," like it was no big thing. I felt so relieved. He even recommended some groups where I could meet other gay kids.

I felt nervous about going. What if someone saw me there and my parents somehow found out? But after a few weeks I worked up my nerve.

I started going to meetings for gay kids in the school and took in some of their positive energy. The kids I met were good people. None of them were rich or freaky looking. They were just "normal." Going to the groups, hearing the other kids' stories, and just being there made me stronger.

Since going to the groups, I've been able to slowly accept my sexuality. It's how I am and I can't change that for anybody.

Accepting the truth has made me more comfortable with myself. I accept that I am bisexual. I am sexually attracted to girls and guys, and that doesn't make me perverted or weak.

Two months after I'd talked to my teacher, one of my closest friends noticed that I'd been talking to the gay kids at school and asked me if I was gay. And this time I said, "No, I'm bisexual." She had the same reaction as my teacher: calm acceptance. It was a big relief, since I was taking a shot in the dark. I told some of my other friends who I trusted most that I was bi. Even though I knew I could trust them, I made them swear not to tell. And again, to my relief, they were comforting and extremely cool about it.

I'm still not out except to a handful of people I can trust. It's nobody's business anyway. The day when I choose to be out is my decision.

In the end, I'm glad I saw Miguel and confronted my feelings. It wasn't easy having that crush. I felt so stupid and embarrassed that I couldn't control my reactions around him. Even now, more than two years later, I still remember what kind of candy bar he had in his hand the first time I saw him.

It was a hard time for me, because my feelings were so new and confusing and scary. This was my sexuality that I was dealing with, and I wasn't ready to be open to it because of my upbringing.

I am more OK with my sexuality now. I'm not sexually active at this point because I want to make sure I'm comfortable with myself fully before diving into a relationship. But I don't question myself about it anymore. I know who I am. And most important, I'm not afraid of that.

The author joined the armed forces after high school.

You can see the actor Mauricio Alexander perform this story at: www.youthcomm.org in the Screening Room.

Stephanie Wilson

My Gay Priest

By Russell Castro

"Holy cow, is that—?"

Right in front of me, in a magazine article, was a photo of my former parish priest Father Jim. He was part of an article about gay priests who were "coming out of the closet"—making public their homosexuality. I read and reread the article just to make sure I wasn't confusing him with someone else.

Later that day, I got a phone call from my friend Will. "Man, did you see Father Jim?" Will said. "How could he do that?"

That night, I showed my parents the article to see their reaction. "How shameful," said my very religious mother. My father echoed her, saying, "You can't trust anyone nowadays." They were astonished that a priest they knew could be gay, as if he was a traitor to his parish.

The next day I shared my finding over lunch with my friends

who knew him from elementary school. Despite all the good memories we had of Father Jim, my friends seemed to forget the man he was. They acted as if he was "insane" and "disgusting."

"Man, all of them cats in the Church are gay," said one of my friends. "They all live together with no women. It's almost like prison, man. They find the next best thing."

"I remember seeing him at one of the school's basketball games. He was probably thinking of getting with the ball boy," joked another one.

"Yo, what about Mass? I bet he was checking out the altar boys," joked yet another.

"That didn't happen," I said. But I soon settled with the reality that in their "Handbook of Manliness," sticking up for a gay guy would, in turn, make me "gay." Plus I didn't want to hear ongoing remarks like, "Hey Russell, another priest's been caught playing with little boys. You going to stick up for him too?"

Even though I thought their comments were unfair, I wasn't sure how to react to Father Jim's revelation. Usually it was no big deal to me to find out that someone was gay. A kid I'd grown up with in elementary school had recently come out and it didn't faze me. But this was a priest, one of the guys who was supposed to be committed to God and no one else, especially another man.

For most of my life, I'd had a Catholic education where homosexuality wasn't condoned. Once when I was 11, someone in class asked a priest about his views on homosexuality.

"A plug and a plug don't fit," he said. "An outlet and an outlet don't fit. But a plug fits into an outlet. Enough said."

I didn't agree with his stance, mainly because he didn't answer why it's supposedly wrong. Isn't God supposed to love everyone despite our differences? But I didn't question it either, not considering the subject to be of much importance.

As I grew older I learned more about gay people, which

disproved some stereotypes I'd had. I'd once thought all gay men were effeminate, loud, and overdramatic, but I was wrong. I met gay people at basketball games and hip-hop poetry slams, and based on how cool they were, I saw there was no reason to treat them differently than others. Plus, I think anyone who acts responsibly should be able to pursue whatever lifestyle they wish.

Still, Father Jim's coming out caught me off guard. I couldn't help but question whether I should condemn him for being gay. Having friends and family damn his actions made me think, "What if they're right?"

Finding out that Father Jim was gay didn't make either of us less Catholic.

I began to think that maybe his homosexuality was wrong because priests just aren't supposed to be gay, just like they aren't supposed to take advantage of little children. I struggled with the idea. I hated the thought of people being unfairly treated because of their differences, but here I was questioning whether someone's sexuality should make me think less of him.

Over the next few days, I reflected on what I remembered about him. I first met Father Jim at my elementary school, Our Lady of Lourdes. He was the associate pastor of the parish.

As children in 2nd and 3rd grade, my friends and I grew to know him as one of the more laid-back priests. Unlike the more uptight, conservative priests I'd come to associate with Catholicism, Father Jim was like "one of the guys."

He gave me my first confession. I was 7 and scared about having to confide my sins to someone I didn't know well. Sitting down face to face with him, I stuttered, "Um… uh… I'm sorry for… um…"

Noticing the Syracuse University basketball sweatshirt I had on, he calmly said, "So, how about those Orangemen," referring to Syracuse's team.

From there we talked about basketball, and I felt relaxed enough to open up about my sins. After being worried that I'd burn in the fires of hell because I'd flipped the bird and used profanity, I left the confessional feeling good that I got my sins off my chest.

Father Jim, with a smile and warm handshake, was a cool guy. He wasn't judgmental about my sins like I'd expected him to be. As a result, I felt more comfortable with the confession process and was able to see that not all priests were going to condemn me for every little indiscretion.

Father Jim was also one of the first religious people I'd grown to admire because he created an easygoing atmosphere to talk openly about anything. If we asked about the significance of a certain aspect of our faith, like Communion, he wouldn't dismiss our question with a quick, "Jesus did it, so we have to do it too," like other priests did.

He gave us straightforward answers and even went so far to say that he at times questioned longstanding institutions of the faith. He made me feel that questioning was a healthy way of better understanding religion.

Unfortunately, Father Jim's guidance was short-lived. When I was 9 or 10, my friends and I were told that he was taking a short break from the trials of being devoted to God. The other priests treated his absence as though he'd soon return.

After reading the magazine article, I learned that he'd taken the leave of absence to live with his partner. Homosexuality is a very touchy subject in the Catholic Church, and I guess I don't blame the other priests for wanting to keep Father Jim's sexuality in the closet.

Despite his short time with us, Father Jim left a strong impression on my friends and me. But it's funny how quickly people choose to forget certain things. My guy friends were so consumed with holding up a certain image of masculinity that they shunned a great human being just because of his sexuality.

My parents and other older people seemed to think Father Jim's homosexuality was a crime. But he hadn't been accused of sexually molesting any children and didn't take advantage of anyone. Instead, the man had enough integrity to leave a profession where he had spent most of his life to be true to himself.

Over the next few weeks after Father Jim's revelation, I stopped thinking about it much. But then I came across the same magazine article that had first caught my attention, and I thought again about how I'd reacted. I felt guilty of blowing the issue out of proportion. Enough time had passed for me to get over my shock. He's gay. So what?

I felt stupid about all of my previous doubts. Why should I let his gayness overshadow what I learned from him? Finding out that Father Jim was gay didn't make either of us less Catholic. If anything, it led me to develop a greater appreciation for his honesty and what he'd taught me.

Father Jim's disclosure also brought me to a better understanding of myself and just how open-minded I thought I was. I try to be accepting of others, but when I think about how I first reacted to finding out he was gay, I see I'm still prone to moments of ignorance.

My eyes have been further opened to the reality that anyone could be gay and that it doesn't take away from who they are. Maybe one day I'll be able to stick up for Father Jim without worrying about getting picked on. At least I can still appreciate the times he was with us, before he was the subject of mean jokes, when he was just "one of the guys."

After graduating from high school, the author
attended Fordham University.

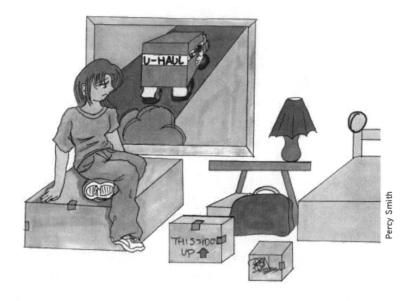

Percy Smith

Kicked Out Because I Was Gay

By Shameek Williamson

During my first four years in foster care, I was in nine group and foster homes. My ninth home was different from the others because I had just "come out" as a gay person and I was worried about being accepted by my new foster mother, Sharon.

When I first moved in with Sharon and her two biological daughters, I kept to myself. I felt close to Sharon but not close enough to tell her I was gay. Since I had just come out, I wasn't sure if this was who I really was or if it was only a "stage" I was going through. I didn't want to tell Sharon until I was sure I was gay.

Before I moved in with Sharon, I came out to my social worker. She thought Sharon would be an excellent foster parent because Sharon had once been in the system, was young, and could probably accept my sexual identity.

After I moved in with Sharon, I used to go gay clubs by myself or with my friend Carla (who was also gay). I wasn't in a relationship yet and this was my way of exploring the "gay scene."

One night at a gay club, Carla introduced me to her ex-girlfriend Bridgette. We only said hello, but I thought about Bridgette throughout the rest of that night and continuously through the week.

The next week I went to another gay club by myself and saw Bridgette. We danced, drank, and at the end of the night exchanged numbers. But because I had just come out, I felt uneasy about having a relationship with another woman.

But after about two weeks of talking on the phone, we decided to go out. We first went to a restaurant and, during the next couple of months, Bridgette took me to get my hair done and brought me flowers, basically treating me like no man ever had. By now I knew that being gay was who I really was.

Sharon, who had been worried because I didn't have any friends, became so happy I now had a friend like Bridgette that she encouraged us to see more of each other.

But even though I was sure I was gay, I still had to hide it from my foster mother. Even though Sharon had mentioned to me that she had gay friends, I wasn't sure if she would accept me because I was living in her home. (Some people think it's okay to have friends who are gay because all friends do is hang out together, but having them live in their house is different because many people believe that gay people are sex-crazed and jump on everyone who passes by.)

One time Bridgette and I went out and she brought me flowers. When I got home, Sharon saw the flowers and said to me, "You told me that you were going out with Bridgette, but you two went out with guys and he brought you flowers." Nervously, I just agreed with her, wondering how long this charade would last.

Somehow or other Sharon eventually found out that Bridgette was gay and assumed that I was gay also. To this day I really don't know how she found out. (Maybe it was the way I whispered on the phone every time Bridgette called, or the way I went into the bathroom to continue our conversations.)

After Sharon found out, she told my social worker that she didn't want me living in her house anymore because she was afraid I would try something with her 12-year old biological daughter. When the social worker told me this I immediately became angry because I would never invade her daughter's privacy in that way.

Moving again didn't bother me because I had moved nine times before that and I had learned not to get close to anyone. So I ended up staying with my uncle for a few weeks until my worker found me a new foster home. I didn't want to stay in Sharon's house if she didn't trust me.

In the meantime, I noticed Bridgette had slowly started drifting away. I asked her why our relationship was ending. She explained to me that she became frightened because she had destroyed a relationship between a mother and daughter. (Bridgette didn't know that Sharon wasn't my mother. I was ashamed of being in foster care, so I had told Bridgette that Sharon was my real mother. Now I couldn't tell her that Sharon was my foster mother because Bridgette would think I didn't trust her enough to tell her the truth from the beginning.)

It's been one and a half years since I left Sharon. Bridgette and I still speak every once in a while, but the relationship is over. Sometimes I choose not to admit it, but I do think I loved Bridgette. I have a hard time admitting it because I try to keep my emotions hidden within myself.

But since that incident, I have been honest at the beginning of my relationships. I tell them I'm in foster care and, if the relationship progresses, I tell them things that happened in my past.

I am presently living with my grandmother. She doesn't know I'm gay because she wouldn't accept it due to her religious beliefs. I can't afford to have her kick me out of the house because I'm 19 years old and there's no place for me to go. But when I do move out in January I might decide to tell her, because I'll no longer be living under her roof.

Being gay doesn't mean you want to have sex with everyone who passes by.

As far as Sharon goes, she was wrong for making me leave because of my sexual preference. I would never have tried anything with her daughter. I would never take advantage of anyone like that. Being gay doesn't mean you want to have sex with everyone who passes by.

Sharon may have had gay friends, but she couldn't accept a gay person living in her home. Personally, I'd rather be moved than live a lie, but no one should have to live like that.

Shameek was 18 when she wrote this story. She later studied social work at Audrey Cohen College in Manhattan.

Jon Kearney

A School Where I Can Be Myself

By Wilber Valenzuela

"Faggot! Queer!"

It was my sophomore year in high school. I had just finished up my last mid-term exam and was heading for the bus when I heard yelling. I turned around and saw a whole crowd of people running after me.

"Faggot! Homo!"

I started running but it wasn't long before they got me. They tried to hit me but a lady driving by in a car started yelling, "The cops, the cops!" The kids disappeared.

That wasn't the first time I was harassed because of my sexuality. My fellow students hurled insults at me all the time. One day I walked into class and saw "Hello faggot" written on the board. I was so embarrassed that day. I was too ashamed to tell anyone about what had happened. I had no friends at that school, no one to turn to. It got to the point where I felt it was wrong to be a homosexual. I used to hide my feelings and keep quiet. I was afraid that anything I said or did would give the others more "proof" that I was gay. School had turned into hell.

Other students had hurt me emotionally many times and I could deal with that. But once I realized that they wanted to hurt me physically, that's when I drew the line. After that crowd of people chased me and I just barely escaped getting beaten up, I was too scared to go back to school. I told a friend about the incident and he said I should transfer to another school. But I figured that no matter where I went, some people would still be homophobic and prejudiced. I didn't know what to do.

Later that week I found out about a support group for gay teenagers called Gay and Lesbian Youth of New York (GLYNY). I went to one of their meetings and told them about what had happened to me. They gave me information about the Harvey Milk School, an alternative high school for gay, lesbian, and bisexual students. I had never heard of it before. I felt relieved to hear that such a school existed. I felt they could help me since I had a lot of questions about myself.

I called the school and they gave me an appointment for an interview. Part of me was frightened about meeting new people, making new friends, and how my mother would react to my decision to go to an all gay school. But I knew I couldn't go back to my old high school and I didn't have any time to lose since I wanted to start the next semester at a new school.

When I arrived for my interview I saw a poster of a group of teenagers and the words, "You are not alone." I had been feeling down and seeing that poster made me feel better. During the interview I had to talk about my reasons for wanting to go to the school and give a brief biography of myself. The next step was a 10-day probation period, during which the staff finds out what your academic needs are and how interested you are in learning.

Harvey Milk was small, with only a few dozen students. Everyone was very friendly and made me feel as if they were my second family. We talked to the teachers on a first name basis, which made us feel closer to them. I liked that I never had to say, "Good morning, Mr. Ashkinazy," but simply, "Hi, Steve."

Everything about the school was different than what I was used to. Since everyone was at a different level, we did a lot of our work independently. My teacher would give me an assignment sheet and a book. After each assignment, I would go to him and he would teach me anything I didn't understand. After three periods of individual classes, we had two periods of group classes. These were different every day and covered topics like health, law, dance, and theater.

For the first time, I felt like part of a community.

Going to the school was like therapy for me. I learned more than just math and history—I also learned about survival. Suddenly my ideas about gays changed. It wasn't like my father had told me. Not all gay men wore leather and tight jeans—that was only the stereotype. At Harvey Milk, all the students were different. Some kids dressed conservatively, others dressed punk. Some were drag queens, but they didn't wear heavy makeup like I thought they would. The lesbians were pretty and not butch.

I also learned about sexuality, AIDS, and safe sex, topics that my other school didn't dare talk about. My teacher and two of my other friends were infected with the HIV virus and they taught me from their experiences. I learned about testing, counseling, and living with AIDS. Safe sex kits were always available.

Going to the Harvey Milk School helped me understand myself and made me more confident about my identity.

For the first time, I felt like part of a community. I felt I could talk to anyone about my feelings without having to hide things or lie.

I also became more aware of the issues that affect me as a young gay man, like gay bashing and the controversy about gays in the military. Now I'm more concerned about these problems and pay more attention to the news and current events.

I also became more outspoken and proud. Back at my old high school, I felt like I couldn't be myself. I remember one day I wore a Madonna T-shirt to school and someone said, "Only faggots like Madonna." I put that T-shirt in the back of my closet and never wore it to school again. But now I feel comfortable wearing T-shirts that let people know who I am, including one that says, "I'm not gay, but my boyfriend is."

I graduated from the Harvey Milk School last June. Going there changed my life and my memories of that experience will live forever.

Wilber was 18 and a graduate of Harvey Milk HS when he wrote this article. He majored in liberal arts at the New School for Social Research in New York City.

Who Was Harvey Milk?

By Wilber Valenzuela

"And the young gay people in Altoona, Pennsylvania and Richmond, Minnesota who are coming out...the only thing they have to look forward to is hope. Hope for a better world, hope for a better tomorrow, hope for a better place to come to if the pressure at home is too great. Hope that all will be all right...and if you help elect...more gay people, that gives a green light to all who feel disenfranchised, a green light to move forward."

These lines are from a speech by Harvey Milk, this country's first openly gay elected official. It gives you some idea of why New York City's high school for lesbian and gay youth was named after him. [See my story on p. 94.] Harvey never forgot how it feels to be gay, young, and unable to tell others.

Harvey Milk was born on May 22, 1930 in Woodmere, New York. He kept very much to himself during his youth. After college graduation, he enlisted in the Navy with the hope that he would help end communism in Korea.

After leaving the service, he moved to New York City. He

started to work in the theatre and that's where he met his companion Scott Smith. In 1973, the couple moved to San Francisco, where they opened a camera shop. The store was on Castro Street which would later become the heart of San Francisco's gay community.

Milk didn't set out to become a gay leader. He wanted to represent the whole community. But his election to the Board of Supervisors (San Francisco's city council) coincided with a growing gay liberation movement. He worked for the passage of a gay rights ordinance in San Francisco and was one of the leaders of the movement that defeated the passage of a new California state law that would have banned gays and lesbians from holding teaching positions in the public schools. He also encouraged other gays and lesbians to come out of the closet.

On November 17, 1978, less than a year after his election, Harvey Milk and San Francisco Mayor George Moscone were assassinated by Dan White, a fellow member of the Board of Supervisors. White had opposed the gay rights ordinance and had unsuccessfully tried to stop San Francisco's annual gay pride parade.

White was found guilty of killing the two men but was sentenced to only 5 1/2 years in prison. The night the verdict was announced Milk's supporters rioted at City Hall.

Milk had believed that he might be murdered. He wrote this poem soon after his election:

I can be killed with ease/I can be cut right down
But I cannot fall back into my closet/I have grown
I am not by myself/I am too many/I am all of us.

If you'd like to learn more, watch The Times of Harvey Milk *(which won the Academy Award for best documentary film) or the Hollywood film,* Milk, *starring Sean Penn. You can also read the biography,* The Mayor of Castro Street *by Randy Shilts.*

Percy Smith

Overcoming My
Fear of Gays

By Sharif Berkeley

I recently moved to a foster care group home in Manhattan. I was looking forward to it, but then I began to have second thoughts because the facility had as many gays as straight people. This was a problem because for the longest time I've been one of those people who teases and slanders gay people.

In the past I hadn't had many run-ins with the people I called "faggots," besides seeing them on the train at night or on TV. To me, they were misfits of society who had serious mental disorders.

I mean, if we're supposed to be the smartest beings on the planet, why do some of us choose to forget what gender we are and what gender we're supposed to be with? Even animals know the difference between male and female, but since we can think, we make up excuses for the things we do.

I was raised to be manly. I was taught that men were supposed to like women, not other men, and the "faggots" were one of the reasons why the world was going to hell.

I've been in various group homes where the residents were all straight. All the guys were always very self-conscious about the way we acted towards one another.

We didn't touch each other too affectionately. We not only made fun of gays constantly, but also of the residents who stayed in the bathroom too long (we used to say they were bustin' nuts). It was all part of being a guy. You had to walk like a guy, talk about girls who have big body parts, and make fun of "faggots."

But now, in my new group home, the tables were turned on me because I had to live right in the middle of the people I made fun of. I thought all the gays would want to touch me (and do other kinds of things to me that aren't fit to print in this article).

On my first day there, I was given a personal tour of the group home. The staff showed me the dining room, lobby, and such. Then they took me to the upper floors where the residents lived and showed me their rooms. (This was the eye-opening part.)

As we roamed through the rooms of the residents, who were not home at the time, I was awestruck by pictures of muscle-bound men and male models lining the walls. I thought to myself, "If this isn't sick, I don't know what is."

Later on I actually saw a group of gay residents. Some stopped what they were doing and gave me this, "Is this the new addition to our group?" look. Somehow I knew what they were thinking when they looked at me. It made me a bit nervous, so I moved on about my business.

During my first week I kept thinking, "If any of these fags

touches me or even looks at me, I'll beat them straight." Beyond that, my attitude towards the whole situation was, keep to myself, speak only to the straight residents, and stay out of the house by keeping myself busy with work.

I was intimidated because I felt that if I did the slightest thing, like brush up against them or even look at them, they would think that I was gay, too. I stopped doing impressions of gay people and my ghetto girl impressions. A few of them started to say that I was gay because I kept to myself.

The concept of someone being gay was inconceivable to me. It was like putting two and two together and getting five. Some of them acted as if they were women with wigs on, and some would run after each other screaming. I would also overhear some of them referring to each other as "she," then talking about themselves like girls do in school.

Just when I thought I had seen it all, I saw a gay resident with permed hair, hazel contacts, and a denim skirt with a pink spandex tank top. At that moment I began to think that I was living in Big Bob's Side Show Extravaganza.

Events such as these were as common as milk on cereal. Every day seemed to be more weird than the last. And to top it off, even the new manager I had at work turned out to be gay. I felt surrounded like a thief in a botched-up bank robbery.

Time after time I thought to myself, "If I could move out of here I would, because I can't stand being around gay people. But if I move out I'll lose out on my college benefits."

And I didn't want to move back in with my family because the problems of my past would happen all over again, and I didn't have enough money to get out on my own.

So as it turned out, I was stuck. There was nothing I could do but live there for the time being.

I didn't think that I could ever come to terms with my prejudice (or "phobia," as one would call it). But eventually there was a slight turn of events which made me put aside the immature feelings I had about gays.

Each day at 12 o'clock everyone came down for lunch. There were about five sets of tables in the dining area. Most of the time I either sat by myself or with people who I knew were straight.

So, one day, as I sat at the table eating, a straight friend came and sat down with me. He didn't have any problems with the gay population and often spoke with them without uneasiness. He lived in the facility way before I got there and had gotten to know them well, even though he admits he felt the same way I did when he first moved in.

As we sat and talked a while, one of the gay residents came and sat down with us because he wanted to speak with my friend. Of course I had nothing to say to that particular person, but the conversation went on. They were talking about a movie they just saw, one I had also seen, so it sparked my attention. I noticed that a lot of what was said and the different topics that were brought up didn't have anything to do with being gay. (I thought that all "they" wanted to talk about were their boyfriends and a construction worker guy on some TV commercial.)

The concept of someone being gay was inconceivable to me. It was like putting two and two together and getting five.

I then started to put my two cents into the conversation. Then another gay resident happened to overhear what we were discussing and came and sat down with us. During the conversation I noticed that I had a lot of things in common with them. We spoke about movies we had seen, stupid things that people did which made us laugh, clothes, and places we liked to go. To my surprise I actually enjoyed the conversation, and I even got a chance to throw in my sense of humor. I got to know a couple of the gay residents and felt a little more at ease being among them.

As the days went on I got to know all of the gay residents

(except one I hated, because he would give me a funny look all the time), and it made me realize that they are decent people just like anyone. They respected my being heterosexual and didn't make comments about my lifestyle or try to influence me.

It took two months, but I've learned to accept who they are and that they can't be changed. The concept of being gay is still something that I don't completely understand and probably never will, but all things in the world are not meant to be understood, so they are best left as they are.

I'm not saying that everything is peachy now, but I have to live among the gay population and I can't see myself hiding and secluding myself. I have to watch how I joke around because I'm still a little self-conscious.

Being prejudiced against people who have done nothing to you is one of the most immature things in the world. I consider myself to be a very mature person, and being prejudiced against gay people was a perfect display of how I could act my shoe size and not my age.

Sharif was 16 when he wrote this story.
He now works in retail sales.

Yam Dor Mui

Breaking Down Barriers

By Melissa Chapman

As a straight teenager, I was a bit apprehensive about attending an all-day workshop on gay issues. The goal of workshop, sponsored by the Lesbian and Gay Community Services Center in Manhattan, was to bring together gay and straight people ranging in age from 13 to 70, so they could break down barriers and misconceptions through story telling, journal writing, and improvisational theater exercises.

I was afraid that I wouldn't know how to relate to the gay and lesbian participants. However, this workshop not only helped bridge gaps in the lesbian and gay community, but also showed me that all people are basically the same, regardless of how they express their sexuality.

As I entered the spacious and brightly lit room, genuine warmth seemed to come from the adults and teens assembled in a large circle. They were passing around a box of folded cards that each participant had previously filled out, expressing their hopes, fears, and expectations for the workshop. Each person had to pick a card and read it aloud to the group, taking on that person's feelings as her own.

One woman glanced at her card and said, "I'm here because my fear as a gay youth is that I won't be heard. I want to have a good time and I guess it's possible to have fun with adults." The room burst into laughter and a sense of unity was forming among the members of the group.

This workshop showed me that all people are basically the same, regardless of how they express their sexuality.

After all the cards were read, each person described her feelings about assuming someone else's personality. One adult said, "I didn't really become another person. Rather, I went back to my own personal experiences. On the card, a teen expressed her fear of being discriminated against in looking for a job because she's a lesbian. As a gay teenager I had the same fears, so I could relate."

After a few more icebreakers, the group became more relaxed. Each person had to go over to someone and find three things they had in common. An older straight woman and a gay teen laughed as they realized what they had in common—a love for men. An elderly man and a teenager were surprised to find that, despite their 40-year age gap, both had been beaten up because they were gay.

"Right now it's hard for me to admit to my family I'm gay," said Hermes Johnson, 17, "but coming to this workshop and meeting with all these well-rounded adults makes me feel more comfortable about my sexuality. And that it's okay for me to be gay."

"After hearing these adults share their experiences," said Eric

Far, 20, "I feel more confident about coming out to my mother."

"I spoke with the mother of a gay son," added Joe Perez, 21, "who told me that sometimes it's not such a good idea to keep my sexuality a secret from my parents, that I should have a more open relationship with them."

"It was really refreshing to meet these kids, who were so up front about themselves. I was impressed with the pride and positive views they possessed," said Sue McConnell-Celi, author of *Lesbian and Gays in Education*, a book in which over 30 lesbian and gay educators present their stories of staying-in and coming-out.

"This workshop reinforced that we've all been affected by lesbian and gay bigotry in some way, youth and adults alike," McConnell-Celi said. "It's important to have open communication and bridge the generational gap."

I feel the only way for teenagers—whether straight, gay, or lesbian—to really understand one another is by abandoning our stereotypes. We should focus on communicating and working with each other as people, realizing that all of us basically share the same fears, hopes, and goals.

The author majored in media and journalism at Hunter College in New York City. She currently writes a column called "Kids in the City" for the Staten Island Advance.

Qing Zhuang

My Place in the World

By Fannie Harris

Last year, a supervisor at my foster care agency suggested I speak on a panel about the experiences of kids in care. In the hallway I noticed a woman with short gray hair wearing a rainbow watch. Her name was Mary Keane. She pulled me aside and asked me to speak on a panel she was hosting on "Being Different."

I've always been different from other kids because I'm black but prefer rock and roll to R&B and rap. So I wasn't surprised that she asked me.

Then Mary asked me if I was gay. Unlike the kids who ask me that on the bus, Mary didn't seem to be asking so she could make fun of me or so she could say something vulgar or rude. I didn't know what to tell her. I said I thought I was straight but that I wasn't sure.

Even though I've always felt different and have been attracted to girls as far back as I can remember, I resisted accepting that part of myself because I didn't want to be gay. Admitting that I might be gay scared me because when I was little, another girl tried to molest me and once, when I was 5, I saw my mom having sex and it felt strange and upsetting to me.

Even so, it was finally dawning on me that I was gay. A few months before, I had gone to the gay pride parade in Greenwich Village in New York City with some friends. I went just for fun (I had never been to the Village before).

The scene was wild and crazy and I loved it. I never knew the gay community was so large and filled with so many different people. A voice inside my head said, "The time to realize my sexuality is now!" After the parade, I thought that there could be no other place in the world where I could fit in and say, "This is me, this is who I am." It turned out I was wrong.

At the panel, Mary told me she was an open lesbian and it didn't bother me because she seemed so normal. Then I met some of Mary's foster kids and soon went to visit them at Mary's house.

The house was huge! It had four floors, 11 bedrooms (some of which aren't even used), six bathrooms, a library, and three living rooms. She had seven kids in the house and there were gay rainbow flags all over the place.

All the kids living there said, "This is the best place I've ever been in." At the time I hated my foster home. My foster mother made me do almost all the cleaning, so I felt like Cinderella. She picked favorites and treated her biological daughter better than me. I wanted to leave there because she made me so stressed out that I cried myself to sleep almost every night. The more I visited Mary's, the more comfortable I felt. "Oh my God, this is my haven," I thought. My inhibitions about gay people started to fall away.

I moved into Mary's house in November. That is when I found a place where I could be my best self, my true self. It felt like living my destiny. About a month after arriving, I stopped caring about what other people thought of my sexuality. I was left with a decision to make—what was my sexuality going to be?

For a while I maintained the straight gig. I didn't quite want to label myself as gay, even though, in my heart, I knew there was a deep reason why I felt so comfortable in this new place.

Mary didn't flaunt her sexuality, so she didn't really influence me in coming out. But the kids…they helped me hit the nail on the head. The kids mainly hung out in the basement, where there's a television. One day a Jennifer Lopez video came on and one of the girls said something complimentary about her rear end. In my head, I found myself agreeing. "OK, there, I made up my mind," I thought. "Telling everybody else is going to be the hard part."

Amanda, a friend of my foster brother and sister, often spent the night at the house. Sometimes I don't notice even obvious things, so when my foster sister told me that Amanda liked me, my reaction was, "Stop lying!" and, "She doesn't even act like she's attracted to me!"

But one night after a party, Amanda handed me a letter telling me that she liked me. She also wrote that it was OK if I wasn't gay, but that she hoped we could at least become good friends. That threw me off. I was shocked and afraid because I didn't know if she was serious or just playing around.

I didn't want to get caught in a love jones that turned out to be a hoax. But the more I got to know her, the more I realized that she was trustworthy. My feelings for her started to grow and grow.

It took about two or three months of continuous letter writing before we actually got to the point where we both understood that we were going to go out. We were pretty much writing about little third grade things like how our day went and how we felt about one another. She was the first girl that I'd ever gone out with.

Dates with Amanda don't really happen much because we're both really busy, but when we do get to spend time with each other it's usually at her house or going to the movies. At first I was a little weirded out by the fact that I was going to be seen holding hands with a girl. But I've had to adjust to a lot of different scenarios in my life, and it only took about a month to get both myself and everyone else used to my relationship with Amanda.

Moving in with a gay parent has given me a positive outlook on what being homosexual is all about.

We express affection toward each other in the same way that any couple would: hugging, holding hands, kissing, and all such. Being with her feels right because my mind and heart say so and I agree with them both.

Moving in with a gay parent has given me a positive outlook on what being homosexual is all about. It's not so much because Mary is gay, but just because of the kind of person she is. You'd have to know her to understand the feeling for yourself.

Mary seems like she's been around since the world began, and when you talk to her it seems like she has the answers to everything. She's also able to handle both parental roles and control all the kids with no problem. She's a role model to me.

So far I've chosen not to talk to Mary about my sexuality, because seeing me with Amanda she already knows. I also don't think it really matters. But I know that, if I ever needed to, I could go up to Mary and tell her something about girl problems and not have to worry if she's going to judge me or ridicule what I'm telling her. I don't have to worry that Mary would take me to church to try to get this "demon" out of me.

I'm emotionally and physically stable in my current situation, and I'm much happier now that I don't have to wake up every morning wondering what sexual orientation I have to pretend to be to please everybody else. Staying at Mary's house reminds me of being at the parade. I'm finally at a place where I belong.

Fannie was in high school when she wrote this story.

I Hated Myself

By David Miranda

By the time I was 11, I already knew I was gay and I hated myself for it. I hated myself so much that I wanted to kill myself. I wanted to be "normal." I didn't want God to punish me and give me AIDS. I didn't want to go to hell.

Every day after school I would go to church.

"Please give me the strength to change myself," I would pray. "Please, please, please." I always expected God to answer me but She or He never did. I remember one day at school one of the kids in my class asked a teacher, "Does God always answer your prayers?" The teacher replied, "Yes, no matter what, in one form or another God will always answer your prayers." Not mine.

I even made a vow that if God would make me heterosexual I would become a priest. After church I would go home and immerse myself in the Bible. All I remember about being 11 is praying. Every Saturday I went to confession. I would confess everything except that I had gay feelings. On Sundays I made sure I went to mass. None of it worked.

"Why me?" I'd ask myself over and over again. I saw myself as a freak of nature, as a devil. All that I knew about gay men were the stereotypes and lies that my parents taught me: that they were child molesters and wanted to be women.

"Siéntate bien," my father would tell me. "Camina como hombre." ["Learn how to sit right. Walk like a real man."] He said these things to me so many times that I can still hear him.

> I felt I didn't deserve to live. I thought about different ways to kill myself.

My parents taught me that gay people were not people at all. Driving through a gay neighborhood I remember them laughing at the "maricas" [Spanish slang for gay men] and trying to imitate their stereotype of a homosexual. This taught me that gay people didn't deserve any respect. So how was I supposed to feel when I discovered that I was gay? How is one supposed to feel when you find out that you are a freak or a pervert?

One day I told my friend John that I was planning to kill myself. I asked him how I should do it. "Why don't you try mothballs?" he said. John was supposed to be my best friend. I figured that if my best friend didn't care whether or not I died, then no one would. I knew that I was alone and that there was no one I could turn to.

That's when I made up my mind to do it. I felt I didn't deserve to live. It was as if there were a knife lodged in my chest that I couldn't take out. I thought about different ways to kill myself. I went to my roof and looked down but I was too scared to jump. I figured that Windex could kill a person, so I drank a whole bottle. It didn't even make me sick.

Then I decided to swallow a whole bottle of Tylenol. I drank it with iced tea, and every time I took another pill I felt glad that I was that much closer to death and that much farther from having to live a miserable life. I closed my eyes and went to sleep hoping it was all over and I'd never have to wake up again.

All I remember from that night was waking up in the darkness every half hour to throw up. I felt as if there was some monster inside of me that just wanted to come out. I remember leaning over the toilet bowl feeling dirty and hearing my father say, "Let it out, let it out, you'll feel better." But I just kept throwing up over and over again.

T he next morning when I opened my eyes, I felt as if I had spent a night in hell. I realized that nothing had changed. I still had to deal with my stepmother who was constantly hitting me, and on Monday I'd have to deal with the kids at school again who called me "faggot."

I went to a guidance counselor and, without telling her that I was gay, told her what happened. I made up a story about a friend dying. By that time I already knew that the best way to keep my secret was by lying.

The counselor called my father and he rushed to school. She told me to step outside while she talked to him. I waited anxiously outside wondering what my dad would do when he came out.

Instead of yelling at me, my normally grumpy father was nicer than I'd ever seen him before. "You're my son and I love you," he told me. "Why would you do something so stupid?" You could tell that he was trying to do everything in his power not to upset me. In a way I was glad because he was giving me a lot of attention. He took me out to eat and talked about moving out of New York City. But in another way it was so fake that it made me uncomfortable.

The guidance counselor told him that I needed to go to the hospital because there was a possibility that the Tylenol could have done physical damage. At least that was the excuse that they gave me to convince me to go to a psychiatric hospital for three months.

I will never forget the fear that went through my mind when they told me I would have to go to a mental hospital. I imagined a place full of crazy people who would try to hurt me. I also imagined a deranged psychiatrist who would put doses of harmful medication in my food.

The three months that I spent at the hospital were actually fun. I woke up every morning and went to group meetings and activities. It was the first time that I actually had friends. Up to that time I had tried my hardest to avoid other people my age. I felt that nobody would like me. I hated people.

At the hospital I was with people who actually liked me. They were all older, about 16 or 17, and to them I was the cute little kid. I enjoyed the way they were treating me. During meals we would talk and I would laugh. I know that doesn't sound like much, but laughing and being happy was a rare feeling for me in those days. At the end of each day we would go to the gym and work out. It was all a lot of fun. And my parents were nicer to me than they had ever been before.

After three summer months I was out of the hospital. I had lied my way through the whole therapy, saying that my only problems were my best friend who had committed suicide, the fact that I had no friends, and that I hated myself. The one time the subject of homosexuality came up I just said, "It's weird. I don't understand how anyone cannot like women." They believed everything I said and sent me to live with my mother in Brooklyn.

In Brooklyn I found new friends. I continued to live a lie, however. One day I went home and swallowed another bottle of Tylenol, for no reason other than to make myself suffer through another hellish night. Another time I took 20 of my mother's blood pressure pills. I felt that I had no reason to live. My vision of myself as an adult was as a lonely, miserable person who would never be accepted by society. The idea of dying in my sleep was very attractive.

I would go to school and chill with my friends and we'd lie to each other about how many girls we'd had. I got into a lot of fights because at that age kids would call each other faggot. I'd get extremely offended by the word and would beat up anyone who said it. Some of my friends would ask, "Why do you get so offended when people call you faggot if you know you're not?"

I would ask myself how they knew what I was or wasn't. I was still afraid to admit to myself that I was gay. I started asking girls out and pretended they were my thing. I started to date them and I enjoyed it. I enjoyed them as far as friendship was concerned but I didn't see it going beyond that.

Junior high school was a total flop for me. I did everything to prove my manhood. I picked fights, got in trouble, and cut school. I went from the class nerd to the most likely to drop out.

I was so afraid of being found out that I stopped going to school.

I escaped when I decided to go to a high school that was outside my neighborhood. All of my "friends" were going to the neighborhood high school, so I now had the chance to go and make new friends in a place where nobody knew anything about me.

On my first day a question was haunting me: "What if people find out?" I was terrified.

At first I made many friends but then I would close up and stop talking to them. I was so afraid of being found out that I stopped going to school for a while just so that I didn't have to deal with people. When I returned I started monitoring my every move. I was scared to talk, walk, or even look at anyone. I felt as if I had the word "faggot" stamped on my forehead. Eventually I was put in truant class. I was just waiting for my 16th birthday so that I could drop out.

I t was during high school that I found that I needed a place to meet other gay people. I knew there were places like that out there, but I didn't know how to get in touch with them. I decided that I was going to ask a guidance counselor for places to go. I wasn't sure whether it was the right thing for me to do. I thought about it for weeks. What if he called my parents? What if he laughed at me? What if they threw me out of school?

Finally I arranged to talk with a guidance counselor. My heart raced and my palms were sweaty as I prepared to tell the first person ever about my big secret.

"How can I help you?" asked Mr. Smith, my guidance counselor.

"I have a very big problem," I said. Then came the big bomb: "I think I might be gay."

He just smiled and said, "And?"

My first thought was, "Is this a joke?"

All at once I was relieved and shocked to find that the first person I told didn't freak out. The experience gave me a lot of confidence. It helped me to realize that I was being too hard on myself.

Mr. Smith told me about a program in Manhattan, the Hetrick-Martin Institute for Gay and Lesbian Youth (HMI). At HMI they had an after-school center where I met other gay and lesbian teens. I couldn't believe that there were other people out there who were going through the same thing I was.

At Hetrick-Martin I got to know kids from all over the city and of all races. It didn't matter that everyone was gay. What mattered was that everyone was cool. It was a place where I didn't have to hide who I was and where I could just be myself.

At first I kind of felt uncomfortable being around other gay people. The trouble was that after pretending to be somebody else for so long I really didn't know who I was. The only thing I had thought about since I was 11 years old was what was I going to do about this gay stuff. At 14, I didn't know how to think about anything else.

Then I found that I was not only gay, I also liked to have fun. I liked to go to the movies. I liked to hang out and chill with my friends, and I loved to listen to music. I was smart. I liked to do things that anybody else liked to do. I was a human being just like everybody else—I just happened to be gay. I didn't admit that to myself until I was 14.

It was around this time that I started my first relationship. His name was Chris. I met him at HMI and found that I liked talking to him. We would hang out with our friends, go to clubs, or just chill and talk. I found that with Chris I felt happier than I had ever felt with any girl. Our relationship was totally based on friendship and respect.

Through all of this I was still cutting school and my mom got suspicious about me hanging out late at night. Sometimes I'd come home high on drugs and try to act as if I weren't high. I didn't care about school. My only concerns became clubs, my friends, and hanging out.

Finally my mother got fed up with everything, kicked me out, and sent me to my father's house. She told me I would amount to nothing and that I would be a bum when I grew up.

I hated my father's house. He put so many restrictions on me that I wasn't used to. I had to be home by 11:30 p.m. If I wasn't home he'd yell and scream and let me have it. I hated having to put up with that. It was around this time that I was trying to let my parents know that I was gay. I was fed up with having to lie to myself or anyone else about what I was.

One day I arrived home and my father was sitting on the couch watching TV. It was a Friday night and it was only 10:30. "Where were you?" my father yelled.

"I was out," I told him.

"What were you doing?"

By this point I was quite angry. Who did he think he was to be screaming on my time? I wasn't a little kid, and I was sick and tired of him telling me how to act, what to do, when to do it, and with whom. So I told him that it was none of his business where I was and that he should stay the hell out of my life. That got him very upset and he grabbed me.

"Goddamnit, you're my son," he yelled, "and I want to know what you're doing." He started to cry and demanded I tell him if I was using drugs, if I had a girlfriend, if I had a job. But the question that really hurt me was, "Are you a faggot?" It wasn't so much the question itself as the way he asked me. He had the most hateful look on his face, as if he were literally ready to kill someone.

"Let me get the hell out of this house," I yelled. "I don't want to live here anymore."

"You're not leaving this house until you tell me what you're up to," he said.

"Let me go or I swear I'm going to jump out of that window," I shot back. The window was five stories up, and I meant what I said.

He started to hit me. I was screaming and telling him that I was going to kill him. I was actually very scared. He kept telling me to shut up because the neighbors were listening. I told him I wanted them to hear. I wanted to open the door and leave but he wouldn't let me. I wanted to kill him.

My heart was beating fast and I was gasping for air and crying. I pushed him away, ran for the window, opened it, and was ready to jump. My father grabbed me. He was very afraid. He said that he was very sorry and begged me to forgive him. I told him that it was okay.

The next day was Saturday and my father called me from his job and told me in a really nice way that in the afternoon we were going to the doctor. I asked why. "You know, just to get a check-up," he said. Later in the day he came to pick me up. When we walked into the office the doctor asked me, "So what's the problem?"

"This ain't a doctor," I thought. "This is a therapist." I was upset that my father had lied to me and I was afraid about spending more time at the hospital. The doctor recommended to my father that I be admitted to the hospital. Once I got there they took blood from me, and then locked me up in a glass room with this man who smelled really bad and who kept talking to himself. Then they gave me nasty food.

Later they made me talk to a social worker. He kept asking me what was wrong but I didn't tell him anything. Yet he still told my father that he thought I was gay.

After a few hours I was sent to another hospital just for teens and then, after about a week, I was transferred back to the hospital where I had been when I was 12. My father and mother talked to me about how much they loved me and how they would support me in anything I did.

I felt angry and confused because I had never told them anything or officially "come out" to them—someone else had. I felt bad that my parents had to go through all this. I knew they were sad and that they didn't want me to be gay. To be honest, if I had a choice, I would not have chosen to be gay either. Who in the world would choose to go through all the name calling, all the bashings, and all the other stuff gay people have to go through every day?

In a way I was glad that my parents found out while I was in the hospital because I didn't have to go through the "coming out" experience by myself. I had social workers and other people there for me. We had family therapy where they would put my mother, father, and me with a social worker to talk about what life would be like for me when I left the hospital. It was agreed that I would go back to live with my mother, and a contract was drawn up about what the rules would be.

My parents and I had heated arguments about what school I would go to and about my being gay. I told them it wasn't any of their business who I slept with. They disagreed and said I was just confused and that I would grow out of it. They talked to me about AIDS, trying to scare me into not being gay.

I told them that I already knew a lot about AIDS and ways to prevent getting it. They acted as if I was stupid and didn't know anything. I told them that if I had sex I would always use a condom no matter what the circumstances. I also told them that I wasn't sexually active, which was true. They acted as if I would get AIDS just because I was gay. They were ignorant in so many ways.

My mother and I talked about what my being gay meant to our relationship. I explained to her that I was still the same person and that it didn't matter. My mother told me that she was upset because she was not going to have any grandchildren from me. That made me angry. "Who are you thinking about," I asked her, "you or me?"

After two months I left the hospital and went to live with my mother. I decided to go to the Harvey Milk School, a high school in New York City for gays, lesbians, and bisexuals. Things have gotten a lot better since then. I have plenty of friends and am happy with my life. Coming out to my family was hard, but now that I have I can tell my parents almost anything and they give me all the support in the world. I'm also involved in a lot of political causes. And I'm graduating this month and will be going to college in the fall.

I know now that I didn't really want to die. If I had, I never would have been able to accomplish any of these things. What I really wanted was to live in a world where I wouldn't have to deal with people's prejudices.

David was 17 and attending Harvey Milk High School when he wrote this story. After graduating from college, he enrolled in law school.

Kimberly French / Focus Features

Brokeback Breaks Hearts—and Stereotypes

By David Schmutzer

When I first heard about "Brokeback Mountain" in my English class, my teacher wasn't referring to the 2005 movie that won three Academy Awards. She was talking about the short story by Annie Proulx about two cowboys in love. The story inspired the movie. My teacher told us to read the story and

---

Brokeback Mountain *is an Academy Award-winning film about the romantic and sexual relationship between two cowboys in the American West. It was nominated for eight Academy Awards and won three, along with many other film honors. In this article, David describes his reaction to the film.*

highlight what parts we thought best captured the love between Jack and Ennis, the two main (male) characters. Some people chose lines the characters said, while others focused on explicit sexual descriptions.

When we discussed the relationship between the two men in class, a few kids giggled at the love scenes. One quote that sparked laughter was when Jack says to Ennis, "Why can't I quit you?" I wasn't surprised by their behavior. The students who laughed were still stuck in 4th grade, a time when many kids think being gay is funny and wrong.

I thought "Brokeback Mountain" was a powerful and provocative story. It breaks common stereotypes about gay men—the main characters are masculine cowboys—and it's moving. When the book was turned into a movie, there was a lot of controversy about showing a loving relationship between two men. I felt the movie was something I had to see so I could form my own opinions.

In the movie, like the book, Jack and Ennis meet one summer in the 1960s while herding sheep together on Brokeback Mountain and fall in love. At first they're hesitant and uneasy about expressing their feelings for each other, but slowly they allow their emotions to take over.

After the summer, Ennis (played by Heath Ledger) marries his fiancé, and Jack (played by Jake Gyllenhaal) eventually meets a woman whom he gets pregnant and marries. The men try to deny their emotions for each other for a while, but they can't stay apart.

For the next 20 years, the men continue to meet secretly every few months to quench their desire for one another. They leave their families periodically to continue their love, telling their wives they're going fishing together. Both still try to be husbands and fathers to their families because they want to be straight, but they suffer trying to accomplish that task. And they always return to Brokeback Mountain, the place where they first met.

One scene that vividly stuck out was at the end of their first summer together. It depicts their emotions bubbling up inside them—a mix of loving each other and hating the homosexuality that they've stumbled upon. To express this, they get in a fistfight in order to be manly and not be gay. But their love for one another eventually emerges.

I already thought there was nothing wrong with being gay before I saw the movie. I believe that within 10 years, gay rights will have been recognized and people will realize how ignorant it was to discriminate based on sexual orientation, just like segregation is viewed now. (Of course, there will still be homophobes who linger on in future generations, just like there are still racists today.)

Still, I was unsure how far Ang Lee, the movie's director, would go to show the love between the two men. When I first saw where some scenes were headed, I felt a bit peculiar because gay sex is something that isn't often shown in books or movies.

It's a love story. So what if it's between two men?

But after I saw those scenes, I felt fine. I've always believed that love between two people of the same sex is entirely natural. I thought of the love scenes between Jack and Ennis the same way I think of love scenes between a man and a woman: just part of the movie.

I know many teens, including a couple of classmates at school, are apprehensive about reading a story or seeing a film like *Brokeback Mountain*. They think it's gross because ever since elementary school, the words "gay" and "faggot" have been thrown around as insults. They associate being gay with being lewd and immoral, even though it's as predetermined as being male or female.

I thought portraying gay people as cowboys was a great way to show there's no shame in homosexuality, since cowboys are considered the pinnacle of manliness. The movie will help people dismiss feminine stereotypes about gay men. Jack and Ennis drink and smoke like many straight men do.

Brokeback Mountain was great for many reasons, from the cinematography to the acting to the costume design. I recommend it to anyone, especially someone who's uncomfortable with homosexuality. Reading the short story or seeing the movie could make you think twice about your feelings. It's a love story. So what if it's between two men?

After graduating from high school, David enrolled at the University of Chicago.

Sarah Evans

Erasing Hate

By Paul Uhlenkott

When I came out as a gay person, I felt so different from the gay people I'd seen on television and in the media. I didn't have a "gay accent" or a "gay fashion sense" or anything else the stereotypical gay man had. I had the misconception that if I hung out with other gay people, I'd be so different from them that I wouldn't belong. That all changed when I went to the True Colors concert last summer.

My mom and I bought tickets because the Dresden Dolls were performing. But a couple of weeks before the show I went online and saw that True Colors was a concert celebrating gay pride, which made me a little nervous.

My mother, who has several gay male friends, wasn't much help. She told me that concerts could get wild. My imagination did the rest. Images ran through my head of people making out in front of everybody else. I already have a hard time with new experiences, especially parties, so I got more and more worried about the concert. I felt I would have to defend not only myself but also my mother from wild craziness. But in the end my mother said we were going—large social events, in her view, are unavoidable parts of life.

When we got to the Greek Theatre where the concert was held, they gave us purple rubber bracelets that said "ERASE HATE" and listed a website, "www.MatthewShepard. org." I hadn't heard of Matthew Shepard and figured they were promoting some kind of business. But I liked the bracelet's purple color and rubbery feel, so I wore it.

As we entered, I was surprised that much of the audience looked nothing like the gay stereotypes portrayed in the media. There were big, burly men who seemed as straight as rulers, but they had their arms around other men's shoulders. There were feminine and petite women talking to their girlfriends. On TV and in movies gay men are skinny, talk like Valley girls, and wear incredibly tight clothes. Lesbians are all butch—they have large bodies, short hair, and pierced noses and ears. I felt more at ease that a lot of the people were like me—not flamboyant, but wearing jeans and T-shirts.

The first band sounded pretty good. If the crowd got out of hand later on, at least the music would be worth it. Margaret Cho, a comedian who's big in the gay community, performed between acts. You wouldn't want little children to hear her jokes. She swore a lot, and talked about sex toys and her sexual habits. It freaked me out hearing these jokes while sitting next to my mother. But seeing my mom laughing helped me relax and enjoy myself. It amazed me that Cho felt free and open enough to joke about those subjects. I couldn't have done what she did, even in a small group of friends. You could tell everyone loved her by the way they yelled and laughed at everything she said. When Cho described her perfect female lover, the two women next to us yelled, "Call me!"

When she finished, the Dresden Dolls, who were the main reason we came, were ready to play. Overall, the performance was good, not great. The lesbian couple next to me drank wine and started making out. This embarrassed me at first but then became charming. I liked that they could show their affection in public and not be judged. I was thankful my mom had encouraged me to come to a place where I could kiss another man if I wanted to, and receive the same respect straight people do.

After Deborah Harry from Blondie performed, Rosie O'Donnell did a hilarious comedy act. She told jokes about her size and her life as a lesbian with children. She talked about how she picked up her son from daycare, and her son's friend didn't understand why her son had two mothers. He said that

> The lesbian couple next to me drank wine and started making out. This embarrassed me at first but then became charming.

his parents were gay, but his friend didn't understand. Then Rosie's son said, "You know how when you hook up the trains, and there's one that just won't hook up no matter what you do? That one is definitely gay." Everybody loved her and screamed out her name during the whole thing. The audience was so light-hearted and open about being gay, which was something I was usually hesitant to mention. It felt nice that there was a sacred space where gay people could express themselves so freely.

Everybody stood when Erasure, the 80s electronic pop band, took the stage next. As soon as they began playing, everybody cheered and started dancing. The girl next to me moved like she had just suffered a stroke and kept hitting me in the face with her rainbow boa, a feathery, light scarf. As for the band itself, I loved the music. The electronic beats and singing were fast-paced and fresh.

I eventually started dancing, something I'd never done in public before. I felt embarrassed because I had no idea what I was doing. Eventually I got over my uneasiness, closed my eyes, and did whatever felt right. I figured that if I could do something as bold as come out of the closet, then a little embarrassment from dancing was no big deal. Besides, some people danced worse than I did but nobody seemed to judge them or care how they looked. I had so much fun that time flew by and soon Erasure was done playing.

Margaret Cho told more jokes and then Cyndi Lauper took the stage. A screen showed slides about hate crimes against homosexuals, including teens brutally attacked by their peers. First there would be a family photo or picture of the crime scene, followed by the person's name, age, where they lived, and a description of what happened. I could hear the crowd gasping. A lot of the victims were killed on the spot or later died from their injuries. I had heard of crimes like this, but at that moment it became much more real for me. The slides were shocking and disgusting, and anger boiled inside me. I couldn't stand the thought that somebody could do such terrible things to somebody else, just because they loved someone of the same gender.

When the screen faded out, Cyndi told us the story of Matthew Shepard, a 22-year-old man from Casper, Wyoming who was tied to a fence, beaten, and left to die just because he was gay. His parents started an organization called the Matthew Shepard Foundation, which has been trying to get a bill passed that would extend the meaning of "hate crimes" to gays, transgenders, and people with disabilities. This would mean more severe punishment for people who attacked gays and more police time in tracking down those who committed such acts.

Though I was glad to hear of the proposed law, I was angry that it was taking so long to get passed and facing so much opposition from religious conservatives. Some religious leaders have argued that such a law would discriminate against their beliefs because they think homosexuality is a sin. Then Cyndi said something that changed my angry feelings.

"Erase hate."

Everybody around me fell silent. So simple, yet the thought never came to my mind. The crowd that was rowdy 10 minutes ago was now subdued.

Erase hate. If I didn't let go of my hatred, would I be any better than those who hated me?

Erase hate. I realized it's not about what other people do. It's about what I can do to make sure the past is never repeated. By not wasting my energy hating any kind of person, I could put that energy to something greater. I could become a better person than the haters ever could be.

It doesn't matter if I'm gay. Sure, it's a part of who I am, but it's not the whole portrait. I have ambitions and fears and loves just like anybody else. A lesser person would focus on hate and allow it to become them, but I decided then and there that I would not become this lesser person. I realized that's what brought us together. It didn't matter that we were gay or young or old—what mattered was that we are all real, unique people, and anybody who couldn't see that just didn't get it.

On the way home I told my mother how wonderful it was to be around other gay people. Although I felt uncomfortable a few times, I told her that I also felt at home, like at a family reunion with all of her crazy cousins. Though I always knew that I wasn't the only gay person around, it felt reassuring to see physical proof by the hundreds. I left feeling pride in who I am, so the concert definitely did its job.

The Author graduated from Hamilton High School in 2007 and is currently attending Sonoma State University in California.

This article originally appeared in LA Youth *(layouth.com) © 2008. Reprinted with permission.*

Ruda Tillett

Finding My Father

By Dominick Freeman

I had a fantasy of what I wanted in my dream dad.

He would know how to make money and help me figure out how to have a successful career as an architect. He would understand that my past, which includes being beaten, humiliated, neglected, and rejected, was not my fault. My dream dad would listen and have patience with me. He would love me and respect me and I would love and respect him back. He would be there for me, forever.

I wanted a man in my life, a father figure, because I never had one. My real father left my mother before I was born. According to relatives on my mother's side, he was a gang member who gave me 22 other half-brothers and sisters.

I desperately wanted to be adopted. But I had been free for adoption since I was 8 and my first two adoptions had failed. At age 9 I was supposed to be adopted by a nice guy called Dave, but his other adopted son didn't want me to move in.

When I was 10, my aunt Sandra and my uncle Willie, who surrendered me to foster care at age 6 due to family tension, said they would adopt me, but because they lived in Pennsylvania and I was in foster care in New York, things got complicated and they didn't. My hopes were raised and then smashed. I bounced from one foster home to another. I never stopped hurting.

When I was 15, I got a clerical job at a hospital for the summer and went to work for Richard Freeman, the associate director of psychiatry. He was a quiet, calm white guy with fewer wrinkles than your average 40-year-old. All the people he worked with talked about how great he was. Richard turned out to be a great boss, because he never yelled at me when I made a mistake.

We left work at the same time, and sometimes, after work, we'd hang out and he'd buy me ice cream or pizza. This made me even happier to have him as my boss.

At the time I met Richard, I was living with a Pentecostal woman in her mid-sixties who devoted all her time to church. She cooked curried goat and white rice with coconut extract and thyme, which I thought was disgusting. A few months after I moved in, I asked her if she allowed kids to swear.

"If you swear at me, I'll send you to another foster home and you'll never come back," she answered.

She told me another kid cursed her, so she called a social worker on him. Two hours later he left and she never saw him again. For this reason and others, I didn't trust her to become my adoptive mother. I never trusted any of my foster parents. I knew they didn't love me and might disappear any day.

My six different foster care placements included a psych ward, a horrible, strict group home, and a home with Mormons who listened to long, boring sermons for six hours every Sunday. The other six days of the week they beat me for stupid reasons with rulers, belts, and brooms.

I was glad I left their house after three years because I didn't want to be beaten to death. I was sick of living with old women and religious people. They couldn't understand why I disliked church, enjoyed rave music and metal, and wore black raver pants.

One day I asked Richard, "Do you go to church?"

"Not in many years," he said. I was shocked because everyone I had ever lived with went to church. "Well, what is your view on religion?" I asked.

"To me, church is a place where people are being controlled by fear. I don't feel that it's right for people to impose their religious beliefs on others," he explained.

That was the weirdest conversation I had ever had. A grown person shared my opinions! This made me want to draw closer to him.

Over the summer, Richard and I took the same train home each night and we got to know each other better. Every day on the train we talked about different political topics: President Bush, the tragedy of September 11th, and our corrupt government. We both agreed that we are liberals. That drew us even closer.

As our conversations became more personal, I let out my past to him and told him how I had been abused. I told Richard that I was in foster care, that I was not adopted yet, and that I would love to live with a dad, or a mom and dad. I had no idea he was actually listening to me when I talked.

One day I went into Richard's office and found him looking at an adoption website on his computer.

"Why are you looking for kids who want to be adopted?" I asked.

Richard said he was researching the topic of adoption and seeing if he was eligible to be an adoptive parent. This made me really jealous. I wanted to yell, "HELLO? Didn't I tell you that I am free for adoption? Why are you looking at all these other kids when you have me?"

Instead, I just told him, "The kids on there are no bargain, you know."

In the last week of working at the hospital, Richard and I got ice cream and sat down in a park. Richard told me about his mother. "Just like you, I had problems with my family. My mother was a person I couldn't stand to be with. I left New York six years ago to go to San Francisco and get as far from her as I could."

That explained why he understood me so well—he had problems with his family, just like I had with mine. Finally I just asked him, "Why don't you adopt me?"

I wanted a man in my life, a father figure, because I never had one.

"Dominick, I want to tell you something," he said in a real serious manner. "I'm gay."

I had chills for a second. I had no idea! He was good looking and could have any girl he wanted. We had talked about our family relationships but not our romantic relationships, so it never occurred to me he might be gay. I had to think for a minute.

"I don't care that you're gay," I finally told Richard. "I just want you to be a good parent to me. That's what I care about the most."

"I'm not going to make any promises," said Richard. "I don't know how long adoption takes or all that's involved, but I will try. I hope one day I will have you as my son."

The week after I finished my summer job, my social worker, William, asked me if I wanted to bring Richard to a baseball game.

When I went to meet Richard at William's office, William walked up close to me, like he wanted to tell me a secret. "I don't know if you know what Richard is doing, but I'll tell you," William whispered. He sounded really, really happy. "He's in the process of adopting you! It's a good thing that you stood up and found a dad all on your own. I'm very proud of you, kid."

I told Richard this and he said, "Well, I was going to keep it a secret, but now you've found out." We laughed through the whole game.

My birth family would never approve of a white, gay man adopting me.

The adoption process started in September with a home visit. I loved Richard's apartment. No roaches and no mice! My other homes had a lot of insects, especially water bugs. Richard had already set up my bedroom. I felt so welcomed when his two cats, Sheva and Thelma, wanted all kinds of attention from me. I'd never been to a nice restaurant like the one he took me to. It was a hell of a good time. What I liked most was that, for the very first time, I got to see how life can be good in New York. Everything was great. This was the right house for me. I wanted to stay as long as I could.

Finally, three days after my 16th birthday, my dad became certified as a foster parent and I moved into his house. Almost immediately, we got into a fight over my curfew, which was 5 p.m. None of my friends had to be home that early. We fought about the curfew for weeks.

Then one day I asked Rich, "If I do what I have to do this month, can I have a later curfew?" He agreed. His acting reasonable made me feel reasonable. For a whole month I came home on time. Richard extended my curfew to 9 p.m. on the weekdays and midnight on the weekends. I was satisfied.

National Adoption Day was a few months later, and that was the day Richard and I went to the courthouse to make my adoption legal. I traded my last name of Gonzalez to become "Freeman." Since that moment, I have become a new man. I feel loved and happy to be out of the system. I'm truly a free man!

Since my adoption, Richard has proven to be my dream dad, but everything has not gone the way I dreamed. Even before the adoption there was tension. I had trouble believing anyone would really be there for me in the long run, so I let out a lot of my frustrations on Richard. When Richard told me not to pour ketchup over all my food without asking or not to interrupt people, I flipped out.

When I decided I didn't want to be on anti-depressants anymore, my dad agreed to let me go off them, but I became much more irritable and slammed doors. I was scared that this adoption could fail like the first two. I also knew it would end all my hopes of being reunited with the family I was born into. My birth family would never approve of a white, gay man adopting me. I tried not to worry so much by reminding myself, "Rich has done more for me and offered me more than everyone in my family put together."

Richard wants me to be more responsible, and he still lectures me about how important it is to care about the people around you. It has taken me a long time to learn how to be selfless. But I am willing to try because I don't want to be self-centered all my life. Families can't work if each person is only thinking about himself.

I had to be self-centered in the past because it was part of my survival—no one else cared about me but me. But now I realize there is no longer any need to behave the way I used to. I don't have to be anxious about being heard all the time, but can concentrate on listening to others. I'm changing.

In the last few months our family has grown. Devon, my dad's boyfriend, and my new brothers, Tyrik, 15, and Derrick, 11, have moved into our four-bedroom house. Derrick, who has a lot of heart and a great sense of humor, is also being adopted by my dad. Tyrik, a foster child who just came into our lives, is also very helpful and supportive. Devon helps us boys with things like cooking and homework and helps keep track of where we all are. I never take my family for granted.

We may not look like a traditional family—we're all guys and all different races—but in lots of ways we are.

I have chores like setting the table, taking out the garbage, and cleaning the bathroom. We go on family vacations to San Francisco, Toronto, Philadelphia, and Boston. Dad takes us away so we can all enjoy different places, but also to advance my education. He has really encouraged my goal to become an architect and is always pointing out differences in city skylines and how buildings are put together. Another difference is I don't have to eat disgusting food. We have food like chicken cutlets, ham, and yellow rice—my favorite!

Also, we celebrate traditional holidays. Christmas is one of the coolest days. Our TV shows a tape of a fireplace, and we have a Christmas tree and hang ornaments.

I can also talk to my dad about anything, including sex. I love to see how much my dad will put up with at the dinner table when I ask him raunchy questions about fantasies or fetishes, but I can also ask him about serious things like love. One time I was in a bad relationship with a girl and depressed because I felt she was controlling my life. At first my dad laughed, but I told him that was very hurtful.

He stopped laughing and said he had been in a similar relationship once and that no one deserves to be manipulated and yelled at. He told me to wait to speak to her until I was calm and to tell her how I felt. His advice helped me handle a situation that could have escalated. My dad is open-minded and sensitive to other people's problems.

My GPA is B+ and I have already been accepted into college. I want to be as successful as Richard. Because he's been my dream dad, in return I want to give him a dream son. Knowing that he will always be there for me, every day, makes me want to make him proud every day, for the rest of his life. I want to be successful, social, and cooperative. For a long time I was a hermit but now I'm feeling a lot more communicative.

The love he has shown me has also changed my opinions of gay people.

When I was little, being called a "gaylord" or a "faggot" was a real bad thing. In care I heard all kinds of negative things about gay people. I was in a group home from age 12 to 14, and because I was physically and emotionally weak the boys there questioned my sexuality and made me feel ashamed that I knew gay people. But living with my dad has made me much more open-minded and tolerant.

I've been way better off having a gay parent in my life than having two straight, abusive parents!

Being gay doesn't make you a good or bad parent. I think what makes you a bad parent is a lack of compassion, and my dad has lots of compassion. I've only told a few of my friends that my dad is gay, because some people assume that gay men molest kids. It offends me when people's heads are in the gutter. I hope that people will change their way of thinking about gays.

For those who think that gay people shouldn't adopt, I have to tell you this: I've been way better off having a gay parent in my life than having two straight, abusive parents! I needed a good parent, and I finally got one.

The author is now attending college in New York City.

Credits

Except where otherwise noted, the stories in this book all appeared in the following editions of *New Youth Connections*:

"I'm Religious, Outgoing, Short, African-American, Talented, Honest...and Gay" by Anonymous, December 1998

"Out, Without a Doubt" by Xavier Reyes, *Represent*, January/February 1997

"She's Cool, She's Funny, She's Gay: My Favorite Sister" by Sandra Leon, June 1992

"My Boy Wanted a Boyfriend" by Ode A. Manderson, May/June 2000

"What Would You Do if I Was Gay?" by Gina Trapani, January/February 1998

"Too Shy to Say 'Hi'" by Eugene Han, January/February 2001

"My Friend or My Church—How Do I Choose?" by Anonymous, November 2004

"Gay on the Block" by Jeremiyah Spears, *Foster Care Youth United*, January/February 2000

"Mom, Dad, I Have Something to Tell You..." by Jose Jimenez, May/June 2003

"Trapped!" by Mariah Lopez, *Represent*, January/February 2000

"Date With Destiny" by Xavier Reyes, *Foster Care Youth United*, November/December 2001

"I Need a Girl" by Destiny Cox, May/June 2002

"Telling My Parents" by Destiny Cox, May/June 2002

"My Crushing Secret" by Anonymous, May/June 2004

"My Gay Priest" by Russell Castro, October 2002

"Kicked Out Because I Was Gay" by Shameek Williamson, *Represent*, November/December 1994

"A School Where I Can Be Myself" by Wilber Valenzuela, December 1992

"Who Was Harvey Milk" by Wilber Valenzuela, December 1992

"Overcoming My Fear of Gays" by Sharif Berkeley, *Represent*, January/February 1996

"Breaking Down Barriers" by Melissa Chapman, June 1991

"My Place in the World" by Fannie Harris, Represent, November/December 2005

"I Hated Myself" by David Miranda, April 1993

"Brokeback Breaks Hearts—and Stereotypes" by David Schmutzer, March 2006

"Erasing Hate" by Paul Uhlenkott, *L.A. Youth*, January/February 2008

"Finding My Father" by Dominick Freeman, *Represent*, November/December 2005

In the following stories, names and/or identifying details have been changed: "I'm Religious, Outgoing, African American, Talented—and Gay," "My Friend or My Church—How Do I Choose?," "Date With Destiny," "I Need a Girl," "My Crushing Secret," "Kicked Out Because I Was Gay," and "I Hated Myself."

The following Youth Communication teen artists' illustrations appear in this edition of *Out With It*:

Shamel Allison
Gabriel Appleton
Elizabeth Deegan
Sarah Evans (*L.A. Youth*)
Mariel Guerrero
Julio Juarez
Jon Kearney
Carolina Moya
Chris Pope
Yam Dor Mui
Jolie Prom
Percy Smith
Ruda Tillett
Kelly Viechweg
Stephanie Wilson
Karolina Zaniesienko
Qing Zhuang

About Foster Care

Some of these stories take place in foster care (also known as "the system"), because the writers were living in either foster homes (with a foster family) or group homes (with other youth) at the time. Young people go into foster care when their biological parents can't properly care for them. Many gay, lesbian, questioning, and transgender kids go into foster care because their families don't accept their sexuality and kick them out. Altogether, about 500,000 young people live in foster care in the U.S.

About
Youth Communication

Youth Communication is a nonprofit youth development program located in New York City whose mission is to teach writing, journalism, and leadership skills. The teenagers we train, most of whom are New York City public high school students, become writers for our two teen-written publications, *New Youth Connections*, a general-interest youth magazine, and *Foster Care Youth United* (now known as *Represent*), a magazine by and for young people in foster care.

Youth Communication was founded in 1980 by Keith Hefner in response to a nationwide study which found that censorship, mediocrity, and racial exclusion had crippled the high school press. Hefner is the recipient of a Charles H. Revson Fellowship on the future of the City of New York from Columbia University and the Luther P. Jackson Excellence in Education Award of the New York Association of Black Journalists. In 1989 he won a MacArthur Fellowship for his work at Youth Communication.

Each year, more than one hundred young people participate in Youth Communication's school-year and summer journalism workshops, where they work under the direction of several full-time adult editors. They come from every corner of New York City, and most are African American, Latino, or Asian. Many are recent immigrants. For these writers, the opportunity to reach their peers with accurate portrayals of their lives and important self-help information motivates them to create powerful stories.

Teachers, counselors, social workers, and other adults circulate our magazines to young people in their classes and after-school youth programs. They distribute 70,000 copies of *New Youth Connections* each month during the school year, and 10,000 bi-monthly copies of *Represent*. Teachers and counselors tell us that the teens they work with—including many who are ordinarily resistant to reading—clamor for these publications. Teen readers report that the information and inspiration in our stories help them reflect on their lives and open lines of communication with parents and teachers.

Running a strong youth development program while simultaneously producing quality teen magazines requires us to be sensitive to the complicated lives and emotions of the teen participants while also providing an intellectually rigorous experience. We achieve that goal in the writing/teaching/editing relationship, which is the core of our program.

Our teaching and editorial process begins with discussions between adult editors and the teen staff, during which they seek to discover the stories that are most important to each teen writer and that will also appeal to a significant segment of our readers.

Once topics have been chosen, students begin the process of crafting their stories. For a personal story, that means revisiting events in one's past to understand their significance for the future. For a commentary, it means developing a logical and persuasive point of view. For a reported story, it means gathering information through research and interviews. Students look inward and outward as they try to make sense of their experiences and the world around them and find the points of intersection between personal and social concerns. That process can take a few weeks or a few months. Stories frequently go through four, five, or more drafts as students work under the guidance of their editors, the way any professional writer does.

Many of the students who walk through our doors have uneven skills, as a result of poor education, living under extremely stressful conditions, or coming from homes where English is a second language. Yet, to complete their stories, students must successfully perform a wide range of activities, including writing and rewriting, reading, discussion, reflection, research, interviewing, and typing. They must work as members of a team and they must accept a great deal of individual responsibility. They learn to verify facts and cope with rejection. They engage in explorations of truthfulness and fairness. They meet deadlines. They must develop the audacity to believe that they have something important to say and the humility to recognize that saying it well is not a process of instant gratification, but usually requires a long, hard struggle through many discussions and much rewriting.

It would be impossible to teach these skills and dispositions as separate, disconnected topics, like grammar, ethics, or assertiveness. However, we find that students make rapid progress when they are learning skills in the context of an inquiry that is personally significant to them and that they think will benefit their peers.

Writers usually participate in our program for one semester, though some stay much longer. Years later, many of them report that working here was a turning point in their lives—that it helped them acquire the confidence and skills that they needed for success in their subsequent education and careers. Scores of our graduates have overcome tremendous obstacles to become journalists, writers, and novelists. Hundreds more are working in law, teaching, business, and other careers. Many former Youth Communication teen staffers have made careers of writing, including National Book Award finalist Edwidge Danticat (*Krik? Krak!*), novelist James Earl Hardy (*B-Boy Blues*), writer Veronica Chambers (*Mama's Girl*), and *New York Times* reporter Rachel Swarns.

For information about our publications and programs see www.youthcomm.org. Contributions to Youth Communication are tax deductible to the fullest extent of the law.

Index by Topic

Dating

Foster Care

Gay Parents (foster—adoptive)

Gay Peer Groups

Gaybashing—harassment

Media—Movies—TV

Overcoming Self-Hatred

Reactions from Siblings

Reactions from Straight People

Religion

School

Therapy

Transgender Issues

Acknowledgments

This book would not be possible without the teen writers who brought it to life and the adult editors who helped them learn the skills to tell their stories. In addition to the editor of this anthology (listed on the cover), the other editors whose writers contributed to this book are listed on the copyright page. Each of them helped writers through 10 or more drafts of these stories—and often guided them through difficult personal journeys at the same time.

Most of the teen writers have chosen to put their names on their stories, but for a variety of reasons several of them asked to remain anonymous. Though times have changed since the first edition of this book was published, they have not changed enough to make all of the writers feel secure in "coming out" and taking the credit they deserve for their stories. We deeply appreciate the contribution of each of the writers, named and unnamed.

Acknowledgments from the First Edition

This is the second edition of *Out With It,* following a successful first edition that was published in 1996. That edition was co-edited by Youth Communication editors Phil Kay and Andrea Estepa, along with Al Desetta. Though most of the stories are new, this edition builds on the spirit and contributions of many people who provided support for the first edition.

Special thanks to four financial supporters with a special interest in gay youth who have supported our work for many years: Henry van Ameringen, New York State Senator Tom Duane, New York City Council President Christine Quinn, and the Paul Rapoport Foundation.

The design of the first edition of *Out With It* was donated by Bill SMITH STUDIO, and executed by Ned Campbell. The Keith Haring estate generously provided the cover artwork for both editions.

Youth Communication editors Duffie Cohen, Carol Kelly, Sean Pierre Chambers, and Vivian Louie worked with writers who contributed to the first edition.

Andrew Humm was helpful in countless ways in developing the first edition. Others who provided advice and suggestions included James Earl Hardy, Bridget Hughes, Lenny Jones, Terry Judson, Betsy Krebs-Stein, Gary Mallon, Ann Northrop, Sarah Wilkinson, and Sasha Alyson.

About The Editor

Al Desetta has been an editor of Youth Communication's two teen magazines, *Foster Care Youth United* (now known as *Represent*) and *New Youth Connections*. He was also an instructor in Youth Communication's juvenile prison writing program. In 1991, he became the organization's first director of teacher development, working with high school teachers to help them produce better writers and student publications.

Prior to working at Youth Communication, Desetta directed environmental education projects in New York City public high schools and worked as a reporter.

He has a master's degree in English literature from City College of the City University of New York and a bachelor's degree from the State University of New York at Binghamton, and he was a Revson Fellow at Columbia University for the 1990-91 academic year.

He is the editor of many books, including several other Youth Communication anthologies: *The Heart Knows Something Different: Teenage Voices from the Foster Care System*, *The Struggle to Be Strong*, and *The Courage to Be Yourself*. He is currently a free-lance editor.

True Stories by Teens

Also by
Youth Communication

Starting With I. Foreword by Edwidge Danticat. "Who am I and who do I want to become?" Thirty-five stories examine this question through the lens of race, ethnicity, gender, sexuality, family, and more. Increase this book's value with Free Teacher's Guide. (Persea Books)

In The System and In The Life: A Guide for Teens and Staff to the Gay Experience in Foster Care. Introduction by Gerald P. Mallon. The special challenges of coming out while in care are explored through stories by gay and straight teens and staff. Activities for every story make this book ideal for staff training or independent living classes. (Youth Communication)

The Struggle to Be Strong: True Stories by Teens About Overcoming Tough Times. Foreword by Veronica Chambers. Help young people identify and build on their own strengths with lessons by using 30 personal stories about resiliency. (Free Spirit)

Fighting the Monster: Teens Write About Confronting Emotional Challenges and Getting Help. Introduction by Dr. Francine Cournos. Teens write about their struggle to achieve emotional well-being. Topics include: Cutting, depression, bereavement, substance abuse, and more. (Youth Communication)

Things Get Hectic: Teens Write About the Violence That Surrounds Them. Foreword by Geoffrey Canada. Violence is commonplace in many teens' lives, be it bullying, gangs, dating, or family relationships. Hear the experiences of victims, perpetrators and witnesses through more than 50 real-world stories. (Youth Communication)

www.youthcomm.org

Notes

LaVergne, TN USA
14 September 2010
196952LV00004B/136/P